Study Skills for Learning Disabled and Struggling Students:

Grades 6-12

Fourth Edition

STEPHEN S. STRICHART

CHARLES T. MANGRUM, II

Merrill
Upper Saddle River, New Jersey
Columbus, Ohio

Library of Congress Cataloging-in-Publication Data

Strichart, Stephen S.
  Study skills for learning disabled and struggling students: grades 6-12 / Stephen S. Strichart,
Charles T. Mangrum, II.—4th ed.
      p. cm.
  Rev. ed. of: Teaching learning stategies and study skills to students with learning disabilities,
attention deficit disorders, or special needs. 3rd ed. c2002.
  Includes bibliographical references and index.
  ISBN-13: 978-0-13-714660-4
  ISBN-10: 0-13-714660-4
    1. Learning disabled children—Education (Elementary)—United States.   2. Learning disabled
teenagers—Education (Secondary)—United States.   3. Study skills—United States.   4. Special
education—United States. I. Mangrum, Charles T. II. Title.
  LC4704.73.S77 2010
  371.9—dc22

                                                                                2009000010

Vice President and Executive Publisher: Jeffery W. Johnston
Executive Editor: Ann Castel Davis
Editorial Assistant: Penny Burleson
Project Manager: Kerry J. Rubadue
Production Coordination: Aptara,® Inc./Ravi Bhatt
Design Coordinator: Candace Rowley
Cover Design: Diane Lorenzo
Operations Specialist: Laura Messerly
Director of Marketing: Quinn Perkson
Marketing Manager: Erica DeLuca
Marketing Coordinator: Brian Mounts

This book was set in Palatino by Aptara®. It was printed and bound by Courier/Kendallville. The cover
was printed by Coral Graphics.

Pearson Education Ltd., London
Pearson Education Singapore Pte. Ltd.
Pearson Education Canada, Inc.
Pearson Education–Japan
Pearson Education Australia PTY, Limited

Pearson Education North Asia, Ltd., Hong Kong
Pearson Educación de Mexico, S.A. de C.V.
Pearson Education Malaysia Pte. Ltd.
Pearson Education Upper Saddle River, New Jersey

Merrill
is an imprint of

www.pearsonhighered.com

10 9 8 7 6 5 4 3 2 1
ISBN-13: 978-0-13-714660-4
ISBN-10:   0-13-714660-4

Introduction

This fourth edition of *Study Strategies for Learning Disabled and Struggling Students: Grades 6–12* provides activities across 12 units of instruction. The units can be used in any order, but the activities within a unit should be used in the order presented. The activities can be used as the curriculum for a study skills class or to improve the skills of individual or small groups of students. The first eight units provide comprehensive coverage of specific study skills. The final four units provide coverage of important support skills.

Here is a brief description of each unit.

Unit 1. Good Studying.

Students learn how to establish a good study place, manage their study time, and use good study habits.

Unit 2. Interpreting and Creating Visual Aids.

Students learn how to interpret and create the following types of visual aids: pictograph, pie graph, bar graph, table, time line, diagram, and map.

Unit 3. Reading and Taking Notes from Textbooks.

Students learn how to use the PQRW strategy for reading and taking notes from textbooks. The steps in PQRW are preview, question, read, and write.

Unit 4. Taking Notes in Class.

Students learn about the three stages of notetaking (before class, during class, and after class), how to identify signal words and statements used by teachers, and how to use the fewest words, abbreviations, and symbols to take notes quickly. They then learn how to use a two-column notetaking format, and how to rewrite the notes they take in class.

Unit 5. Using Reference Sources.

Students learn how to use print and electronic formats of the following types of reference sources: dictionary, thesaurus, encyclopedia, almanac, and atlas.

Unit 6. Interpreting and Constructing Graphic Organizers and Charts.

Students learn how to interpret and create the following types of graphic organizers and charts: topic-list graphic organizer, sequence chart, problem-solution graphic organizer, series of events graphic organizer, compare-contrast graphic organizer, question-answer graphic organizer, cause-effect graphic organizer, five W's chart, and KWL chart.

Unit 7. Remembering Information.

Students learn how to use the following strategies for remembering information: rehearsal, visualization, grouping, rhyme, acronym, first letters, acronymic sentence, pegwords, and loci.

Unit 8. Taking Tests.

Students learn how to use the DETER strategy for taking any type of objective test. The steps in DETER are: read the test directions carefully, examine the entire test to see how much there is to do, decide how much time to spend answering each question, answer the easiest questions first, and review answers. Students then learn specific strategies for taking each of the following types of tests: multiple-choice, true/false, matching, completion, and essay.

Unit 9. Reading Long Words.

Students learn how to use the P2SBA strategy to read long (i.e., multisyllable) words. The steps in P2SBA are: look for a prefix, look for a suffix, look for the stem, blend the parts, and ask for help if needed.

Unit 10. Spelling Long Words.

Students learn how to use the syllable-building strategy to spell long words. The steps in the syllable-building strategy are: copy the word, locate the word in a dictionary, pronounce the word, write the word leaving a space between each syllable, write and pronounce the syllables individually and combined, write the word on a personal spelling list as an entire word and broken into syllables, and use one of the three strategies provided to review the spelling of the word.

Unit 11. Building Vocabulary through Reading.

Students learn how to build their vocabularies while reading by identifying and making use of definition, synonym, and visual clues provided by writers.

Unit 12. Solving Math Word Problems.

Students learn how to use the RQWQC strategy for solving math word problems. The steps in RQWQC are: **r**ead to learn what the problem is about; identify the **q**uestion to be answered; **w**rite the information needed to answer the question; identify the computations that must be done to answer the **q**uestion; and do the **c**omputations.

Teacher's Guide

An accompanying online *Teacher's Guide* provides directions for using the activities, ideas for extending the activities, and answer keys. To download the *Guide*, please go to **www.pearsonhighered.com** and click on *Instructor's Resource Center* located on the top navigation bar of the home page.

About The Authors

Dr. Charles T. Mangrum, II earned a B.S. in Sociology from Northern Michigan University, an M.S. in Education from Northern Michigan University, an Ed.S. in Reading Education from Southern Illinois University, and an Ed.D. in Reading Education from Indiana University. Dr. Mangrum taught in elementary schools and high schools in Michigan, and served as a reading consultant in Illinois public schools. He was Professor of Reading Education and Special Education at the University of Miami for thirty five years. Dr. Mangrum also maintained a private practice in which he evaluated several thousand students for learning problems and possible learning disabilities.

Dr. Stephen S. Strichart earned a B.B.A. in Business Statistics from the City College of New York, an M.S. in Clinical School Psychology from the City College of New York, and a Ph.D. in Special Education from Yeshiva University. Dr. Strichart taught special education classes in the New York City public schools. He was Professor of Educational Psychology and Special Education at Rutgers University and Florida International University for thirty three years. Dr. Strichart also maintained a private practice in which he evaluated several thousand students for learning problems and possible learning disabilities.

Dr. Mangrum and Dr. Strichart have published numerous articles and research studies in professional journals, and they have made major presentations at state, national, and international conferences. They have authored study skills, reading, and language arts textbooks and instructional programs for many major publishers.

Contents

UNIT TWELVE
Solving Math Word Problems   223

Good Studying

ACTIVITIES

Good studying involves:

1. Using an appropriate **place** to study.

Write a statement that describes your study place.

_____

_____

_____

_____

2. Managing your study **time** effectively.

Write a statement that describes how you manage your time.

_____

_____

_____

_____

3. Consistently using good study **habits**.

Write a statement that describes your study habits.

_____

_____

_____

_____

Evaluating My Study Place

Read each feature of a study place. If your study place has that feature, place a ✔ under Yes. If it does not, place a ✔ under No.

My Study Place	Yes	No
I can use it whenever I need to.	_____	_____
There are few things to distract me from studying.	_____	_____
There is enough light to see without straining my eyes.	_____	_____
The temperature can be set at a comfortable level.	_____	_____
There is a large enough desk or table.	_____	_____
It contains all the books and materials I need.	_____	_____
It is free from interruptions.	_____	_____
It contains a comfortable chair.	_____	_____
It contains enough storage space.	_____	_____
It contains a computer.	_____	_____

Improving My Study Place

Write each feature for which you checked "No" when completing Activity 1-2. Then write a statement that tells what you can do to improve that study place feature. If you cannot improve it, explain why you cannot.

Feature that needs to be improved: _____

What I can do to improve it: _____

_____

_____

Feature that needs to be improved: _____

What I can do to improve it: _____

_____

_____

Feature that needs to be improved: _____

What I can do to improve it: _____

_____

_____

Feature that needs to be improved: _____

What I can do to improve it: _____

_____

_____

Feature that needs to be improved: _____

What I can do to improve it: _____

_____

_____

You cannot change the amount of schoolwork you are assigned. You cannot change the amount of time there is in a day, week, or month. What you can do is **manage your time** to provide enough time to complete your schoolwork while still allowing for all the other things you have to do in your life.

Here is a strategy for managing your time.

Use a **monthly calendar** for each month of the school year. Enter important events, assignments, and tests on the appropriate monthly calendar as soon as you become aware of them. Your monthly calendars will provide you with a "big picture" of the school year and allow you to plan ahead.

Use a **weekly calendar** for each week of the school year. Prepare your weekly calendar before the beginning of each week. Update it as the week goes on. Your entries should be more specific and detailed than those on your monthly calendar.

Use a **daily to-do list** for each day of the school year. Prepare your daily to-do list each evening before a school day. These entries should be the most specific and detailed of all.

Answer the following questions.

1. What does a monthly calendar provide?

   _____

2. Where should you write your most detailed entries?

   _____

3. When should you prepare a daily to-do list?

   _____

4. What should you enter on a monthly calendar?

   _____

5. What does a monthly calendar allow you to do?

   _____

6. What is the purpose of managing your time?

   _____

Here is how to prepare a **monthly calendar**.

- Record your assignments on their due dates.
- Record your test dates on the dates they will be given.
- Record your planned school activities such as assemblies and field trips.
- Record your planned out-of-school activities such as club meetings, sporting events, and special family activities.

Carry your monthly calendars with you so you can update them as needed. It is a good idea to punch holes in them and insert them in the front of your loose-leaf binder. Or, keep them in the pocket of your notebook.

Think of some entries you would make on a monthly calendar for this month or next month. Write them here:

1. Assignments and tests.

_____

_____

_____

_____

_____

_____

2. School activities.

_____

_____

_____

_____

_____

_____

3. Out-of-school activities.

_____

_____

_____

_____

_____

_____

Write the entries you just wrote on the blank monthly calendar provided with this activity.

Monthly Calendar

Name: _____ Month: _____ Year: _____

SUNDAY	MONDAY	TUESDAY	WEDNESDAY	THURSDAY	FRIDAY	SATURDAY

Preparing a Weekly Calendar

Here is how to prepare a **weekly calendar** before the beginning of each week.

- Enter your classes for each day of the coming week.
- Review your *monthly calendar* for the coming week. Add entries for that week from the monthly calendar to your weekly calendar. Make the entries more specific and detailed than they are on the monthly calendar.
- Check your notes and handouts from the week just ended to see if there are any additional school activities you need to enter for the coming week.
- Check your notes and handouts from the week just ended to see if there are any additional out-of-school activities you need to enter for the coming week.

Carry your weekly calendar with you so you can update it as needed.

Think of some entries you would make on a weekly calendar for this week or next week. Write them here:

1. Entries to add from your monthly calendar.

_____

_____

_____

_____

_____

_____

2. Additional school activities.

_____

_____

_____

_____

_____

_____

3. Additional out-of-school activities.

_____

_____

_____

_____

_____

_____

Write your classes and the entries you just wrote on the blank weekly calendar provided with this activity.

Weekly Calendar

Name:_____   Week of: _____

TIME	SUNDAY	MONDAY	TUESDAY	WEDNESDAY	THURSDAY	FRIDAY	SATURDAY
8:00							
9:00							
10:00							
11:00							
12:00							
1:00							
2:00							
3:00							
AFTER SCHOOL							
EVENING							

Here is how to prepare a **daily to-do list** for the next day each evening before a school day.

- Review your *weekly calendar* for the coming day. Add entries from that day to your daily to-do list. Make the entries more specific and detailed than they are on the weekly calendar.
- Review your notes and handouts for the day just completed to see what things you need to do the next day. Add these things to your daily to-do list for the next day.
- Review your daily to-do list for the day just completed. Add things to your daily to-do list for the next school day you were supposed to do but did not accomplish.

Carry your daily to-do list with you. Cross out things as you accomplish them. Add new things to do as you become aware of them.

Think of some entries you would make on a daily to-do list for the next school day. Write them here.

1. Entries from your weekly calendar.

_____

_____

_____

_____

_____

_____

2. Things to do from your notes and handouts.

_____

_____

_____

_____

_____

_____

3. Things from today and previous days that were not accomplished and still need to be done.

_____

_____

_____

_____

_____

_____

Write the entries you wrote on the blank daily to-do list provided with this activity.

Daily To-Do List

Name: _____   Day/Date: _____

8:00	
9:00	
10:00	
11:00	
12:00	
1:00	
2:00	
3:00	
AFTER SCHOOL	
EVENING	

Evaluating My Study Habits

Read each study habit. If it is something you do all or most of the time, place a ✓ under Yes. If it is not, place a ✓ under No.

My Study Habits	Yes	No
I try not to do too much studying at one time.	_____	_____
I plan specific times for studying.	_____	_____
I tell my friends not to call me during my study time.	_____	_____
I set specific goals when I study.	_____	_____
I start studying when planned.	_____	_____
I review my notes before beginning an assignment.	_____	_____
I begin with the hardest assignment.	_____	_____
I review my schoolwork over the weekend.	_____	_____
I finish one assignment before going on to another.	_____	_____
I take short breaks when I feel tired.	_____	_____
I avoid daydreaming.	_____	_____
I have a "study buddy" I can contact when I get stuck.	_____	_____
I write down questions I will need to ask my teacher.	_____	_____
I keep working on long-term assignments.	_____	_____

Improving My Study Habits

Write each study habit for which you checked "No" when completing Activity 1-8. Then write a statement that tells what you can do to establish that study habit.

Study habit that needs to be established: _____

What I can do to establish it: _____

_____

_____

_____

Study habit that needs to be established: _____

What I can do to establish it: _____

_____

_____

_____

Study habit that needs to be established: _____

What I can do to establish it: _____

_____

_____

_____

Study habit that needs to be established: _____

What I can do to establish it: _____

_____

_____

_____

Study habit that needs to be established: _____

What I can do to establish it: _____

_____

_____

_____

1. What three things does good studying involve?

   _____

   _____

   _____

2. What are five characteristics of a good study place?

   _____

   _____

   _____

   _____

   _____

3. What are the three components of a strategy for managing time?

   _____

   _____

   _____

4. What are five study habits that should be a consistent part of your studying?

   _____

   _____

   _____

   _____

   _____

Interpreting and Creating Visual Aids

ACTIVITIES

Pictograph

Graphs visually show how two or more things go together. A **pictograph** uses pictures or drawings to show information. The title tells you what the pictograph shows. The *legend* tells you what each picture or drawing represents.

Look at the pictograph that follows. The title tells you it shows the number of World Series won by each of a number of baseball teams. The legend tells you that each baseball next to the name of a team stands for one World Series won by that team. You can tell how many World Series each team has won by counting the number of baseballs next to that team's name.

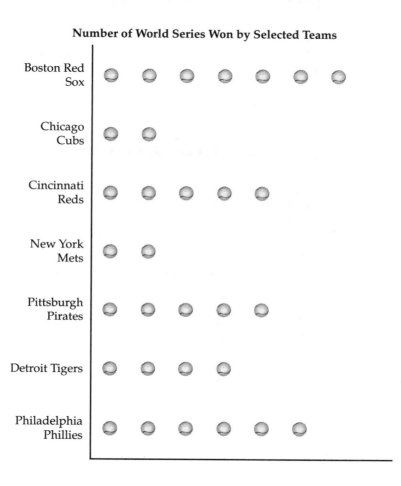

Number of World Series Won by Selected Teams

$\bigcirc$ = 1 World Series

Now look at this pictograph.

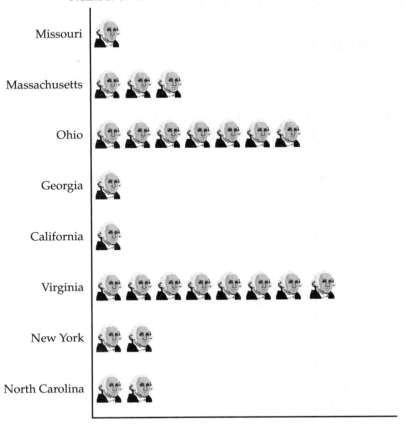

Number of U.S. Presidents Born in Selected States

= 1 President

Answer these questions about the pictograph.

1. What does this pictograph show? _____

2. What does ![] represent? _____

3. In which state were the most presidents born? _____

4. In which states was just one president born? _____

5. How many more presidents were born in Ohio than in Massachusetts? _____

6. Does the number of presidents born in Virginia exceed the number of presidents born in

   North Carolina, New York, California, Georgia, and Missouri combined? _____

7. Create a pictograph to show the following information:

Number of Electoral College votes in selected states:

Arkansas	6	Alabama	9
South Carolina	4	Arizona	10
Georgia	15	Iowa	8
Pennsylvania	21	Indiana	11
West Virginia	13	Kansas	6

Pie Graph

A **pie graph** is a circle divided into parts or segments. It is called a pie graph because it looks like a pie divided into slices. A pie graph is also often called a *circle graph*.

A pie graph uses percentages to show information. Each part of a pie graph represents a specific category and shows the percentage of the whole that category accounts for. Sometimes there is a part called "Other" that combines very small categories that are difficult to show. The parts of the pie graph must add up to 100%.

Look at the pie graph that follows. The title tells you it shows what kinds of things people throw out as garbage.

What We Throw Out as Garbage

7%
Metal

23%
Other

3%
Rubber and
Leather

25%
Paper

24%
Food and Yard
Waste

18%
Plastic

Now look at this pie graph.

U.S. Population by Age (2000)

3%
80 and over

7%
Under 5

13%
60–79

22%
5–19

26%
40–59

29%
20–39

Answer these questions about the pie graph from the previous page.

1. What does this pie graph show? _____

2. Which age group represents the largest percentage of the population? _____

3. Which age group represents the smallest percentage of the population? _____

4. What percentage of the population is under age 60? _____

5. What percentage of the population is over age 40? _____

6. What percentage of the population is older than 19 but younger than 60? _____

7. Are there more very young children or very old people in the population? _____

8. Now, create a pie graph to show the following information.

**Population of Central America
by percentage in 2007:**

Belize	1%
Honduras	19%
Guatemala	31%
Nicaragua	14%
Costa Rica	10%
El Salvador	17%
Panama	8%

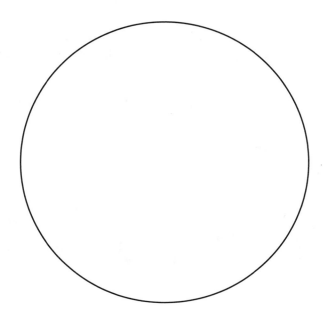

Vertical Bar Graph

A **bar graph** represents data in different categories. Bar graphs may be vertical or horizontal. The title tells what the graph shows.

On a **vertical bar graph**, numbers go up the left side of the graph. A label on the left side of the graph tells what the numbers stand for. The single label at the bottom tells the general category of things represented. The label at the bottom of each bar tells the specific thing within that category that the bar represents. The higher the bar, the greater the numerical value of whatever the bar represents.

Look at the vertical bar graph that follows. The title tells you it shows the required number of players for different sports. The label on the left tells you that the numbers stand for the number of players required. The single label at the bottom tells you that the general category being shown is different sports. The label at the bottom of each bar tells you the specific sport represented by the bar.

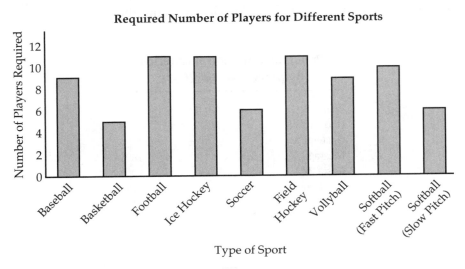

Now look at the following vertical bar graph. Because it is showing data for two different years, each year is represented by a differently shaded bar. A legend tells you which year each shade represents.

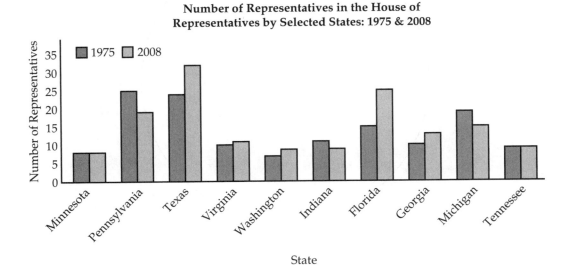

Answer these questions about the second bar graph from the previous page.

1. What does this graph show? _____

2. What does the lighter shade represent? _____

3. How many states are included in this graph? _____

4. How many representatives did Indiana have in 1975? _____

5. How many representatives did Georgia have in 2008? _____

6. Which states showed no change from 1975 to 2008? _____

7. Which state had the greatest growth from 1975 to 2008? _____

8. Which state had the greatest decrease from 1975 to 2008? _____

9. How many more representatives did Virginia have than Tennessee in 1975? _____

10. How many fewer representatives did Michigan have than Florida in 2008? _____

11. Which state had the most representatives in 1975? _____

12. Did this state continue to have the most representatives in 2008? _____

13. Now, create a bar graph to show the following information:

    SAT scores in 2007

State	Critical Reading	Math
Connecticut	510	512
Hawaii	484	506
California	499	516
Wisconsin	587	598
Kentucky	567	565
Tennessee	574	569
New York	491	505
Colorado	560	565
Utah	558	556
Delaware	497	496
Ohio	536	542
Alabama	563	556

Horizontal Bar Graph

2-4

A **horizontal bar graph** is often used in place of a vertical bar graph when the labels for what is shown by each bar are too long to fit along the bottom of the graph. The use of a horizontal bar graph allows the labels to be placed on the left side of the graph, where there is more room.

On a horizontal bar graph, numbers go along the bottom of the graph. A label at the bottom of the graph tells what the numbers stand for. The single label at the left of the graph tells the general category of things represented. The label at the left of each bar tells the specific thing within that category the bar represents. The longer the bar, the greater the numerical value of whatever the bar represents.

Look at the horizontal bar graph that follows. The title tells you it shows the top-selling albums of all time. The label at the bottom tells that the numbers stand for millions of albums sold. The single label at the left tells you that the general category being shown is names of albums and artists. The label at the left of each bar tells the name of a specific album and its artist.

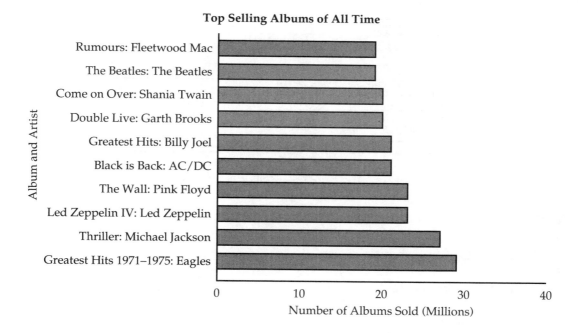

Top Selling Albums of All Time

Now look at the following horizontal bar graph. Because it is showing data for two different years, each year is represented by a differently shaded bar. A legend tells you which year each shade represents.

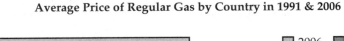

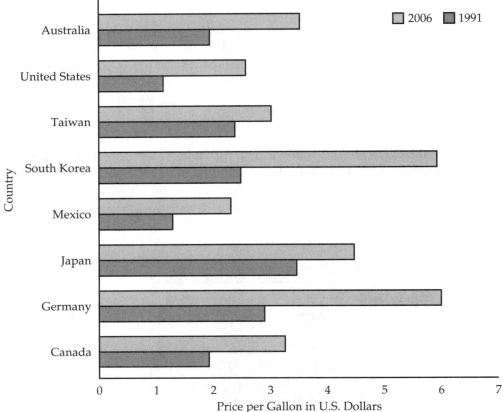

Answer these questions about the bar graph.

1. What does this graph show? _____

2. What does the darker shade represent? _____

3. How many countries are included in this graph? _____

4. What was the approximate price of gas in South Korea in 1991? _____

5. What was the approximate price of gas in Japan in 2006? _____

6. In which country was gas most expensive in 1991? _____

7. In which country was gas least expensive in 2006? _____

8. Which country had the greatest price increase from 1991 to 2006? _____

9. Did the price of gas in the United States more than double from 1991 to 2006? _____

10. Approximately how many gallons of gas could you purchase for $5 in South Korea in 1991? _____

11. Which country had the smallest increase in the price of gas from 1991 to 2006? _____

12. Approximately how much more would a gallon of gas cost in 2006 in Germany than in Mexico? _____

13. Here is the highest and lowest elevation in feet for ten states. Create a horizontal bar graph to show this data.

State	Highest Elevation	Lowest Elevation
Ohio	1,600	500
South Dakota	7,200	1,000
New Mexico	13,200	2,800
Idaho	12,700	700
West Virginia	4,900	200
Mississippi	1,800	200
Michigan	2,000	600
Oklahoma	5,000	300
Wisconsin	2,000	600
Colorado	14,400	3,300

Line Graph

A **line graph** is often used to show information over a period of time. It is useful for learning about something at a specific time, comparing something at different times, and seeing trends over time.

The title tells what the graph shows. Numbers go up the left side of the graph. The label on the left side of the graph tells what the numbers stand for. The period of time represented by the graph is shown along the bottom.

When only one thing is shown by the graph, as is the case for the graph that follows, a dot is typically used to represent a data point. The higher the data point on the graph, the greater the value of whatever is being shown by the graph.

Look at the line graph that follows. The title tells you it shows the frequency of tornadoes in the United States from 1990 through 2000. Because only one thing is shown, dots are used to represent data points.

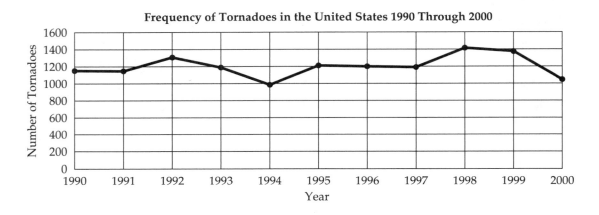

Now look at the following line graph. Note that it shows separate data for elderly men and elderly women. Consequently, a legend is provided to show which symbol represents a data point for men and which one for women.

Answer these questions about the second line graph from the previous page.

1. What does this graph show? _____

2. What period of time is shown by the graph? _____

3. What is the number of years between each data point? _____

4. What symbol is used to represent data for elderly women? _____

5. How would you describe the trend for elderly men in the labor force? _____

6. Is there a clear trend for elderly women in the labor force? _____

7. In what year did the percentage of elderly men in the labor force most greatly exceed the percentage of elderly women? _____

8. In what year were elderly women most highly represented in the labor force? _____

9. In what year was the percentage of elderly men and the percentage of elderly women in the labor force closest? _____

10. Here are the most home runs hit in the National League and the American League from 1995 through 2007. Create a line graph to show this data.

Year	American League	National League
1999	48	65
2001	52	73
1995	50	40
2007	54	50
2000	47	50
2006	54	58
1996	52	47
2004	43	48
1998	56	70
2005	48	51
1997	56	49
2002	57	49
2003	47	47

Table

A **table** shows facts that would be difficult to understand quickly and accurately if presented only as written text. Tables are an excellent way to show a lot of information in a condensed space. The title tells what information the table presents. Each column in the table has a heading that tells what specific information you will find in the column.

Look at the table that follows. It presents several facts about a number of nations in the world.

Facts About Nations (2007)

Country	Population	Population Density	Total Area (square miles)	Arable Land
Argentina	40,301,927	38	1,068,302	10%
Australia	20,434,176	7	2,967,909	6%
Canada	33,390,141	10	3,855,103	5%
China	1,321,851,888	367	3,708,407	15%
Indonesia	234,693,997	333	741,100	11%
Mexico	108,700,891	146	761,606	13%
Netherlands	16,570,613	1267	16,033	22%
Peru	28,674,757	58	496,226	3%
Russia	141,377,752	22	6,592,772	7%
United States	301,139,947	85	3,718,712	18%

Now look at this table.

Average U.S. Television Viewing Time, May 2007
(hours:minutes per week)

Group	Age	Total per week	M–F 7–10 AM	M–F 10 AM–4 PM	M–Sun 8–11 PM	Sat. 7 AM–1 PM	M–F 11:30 PM–1 AM	Sun 1 PM–7 PM
Men	18–24	21:40	0:56	2:51	4:57	0:32	1:26	0:58
	25–54	28:13	1:35	3:07	7:29	0:50	1:36	1:23
	55+	36:48	2:20	4:53	9:53	0:58	1:32	1:51
Women	18–24	26:53	1:31	4:16	6:12	0:41	1:34	1:04
	25–54	32:05	2:16	4:25	8:19	0:53	1:43	1:13
	55+	43:21	3:08	7:01	11:02	1:06	1:46	1:42
Children	2–11	21:40	1:51	3:11	4:45	1:07	0:40	0:58
Teens	12–17	21:20	0:50	1:35	5:39	0:46	1:08	1:02
ALL VIEWERS		30:04	1:57	4:00	7:39	0:54	1:27	1:18

Answer these questions about the table.

1. What does this table show? _____

2. What age range is shown? _____

3. Which group watches the most TV on weekday mornings? _____

4. Which group watches the least TV on weekday mornings? _____

5. When do women 55 and older watch the most TV? _____

6. When do children 2 to 11 watch the least TV? _____

7. When is the most popular time to watch TV? _____

8. Do teenagers watch more TV than elderly people? _____

9. Is Saturday from 7 AM to 1 PM a generally more popular viewing period than Sunday from

   1 to 7 PM? _____

10. Now, create a table to show the following information about the 34th through the 42nd presidents of the United States:

   34th: Dwight D. Eisenhower was born in Texas in 1890. He served from 1953 to 1961. He was 62 when he became president. He was a Republican. Richard Nixon was his vice-president.

   35th: John F. Kennedy served from 1961 to 1963. He was born in Massachusetts in 1917. Lyndon B. Johnson was his vice-president. Kennedy was a Democrat. He was 43 when he became president.

   36th: Lyndon B. Johnson was a Democrat. He was born in Texas in 1908. He served from 1963 to 1969. He was 55 when he became president. Hubert Humphrey was his vice-president.

   37th: Richard Nixon was 56 when he became president. He was born in California in 1913 and was a Republican. He had two vice-presidents: Spiro Agnew and Gerald Ford. He served from 1969 to 1974.

   38th: Gerald Ford, a Republican, served from 1974 to 1977. His vice-president was Nelson Rockefeller. Ford was born in Nebraska in 1913. He was 61 when he became president.

   39th: Jimmy Carter is a Democrat. He was 52 when he became president and was born in Georgia in 1924. His vice-president was Walter Mondale. He served from 1977 to 1981.

   40th: Ronald Reagan served from 1981 to 1989. His vice-president was George H. W. Bush. Reagan was a Republican who was 69 when he became president. He was born in Illinois in 1911.

   41st: George H. W. Bush is a Republican who served from 1989 to 1993. His vice-president was Dan Quayle. Bush was born in Massachusetts in 1924. He was 64 when he became president.

   42nd: Bill Clinton is a Democrat who was 46 when he became president. He served from 1993 to 2001, with Al Gore as his vice-president. Clinton was born in 1946 in Arkansas.

A **time line** shows the dates of important events over a period of time. Time lines can be presented in a horizontal format or in a vertical format. By convention, earliest events are shown at the left of a horizontal time line and at the top of a vertical time line.

Look at this horizontal time line.

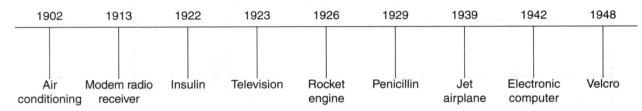

Important Inventions (1900–1950)

1902	1913	1922	1923	1926	1929	1939	1942	1948
Air conditioning	Modem radio receiver	Insulin	Television	Rocket engine	Penicillin	Jet airplane	Electronic computer	Velcro

Now look at the following vertical time line.

Important American Firsts

1635	Public school	Boston Latin, Boston MA
1636	College	Harvard, Cambridge, MA
1716	Lighthouse	Boston Light, Boston, MA
1752	Hospital	Pennsylvania Hospital, Philadelphia, PA
1773	Public Museum	Charleston Museum, Charleston, SC
1781	Bank	First Bank of the United States, Philadelphia, PA
1784	Daily Newspaper	Pennsylvania Packet and Daily Advisor, Philadelphia, PA
1885	Skyscraper	Home Insurance Building, Chicago, IL
1893	Ferris Wheel	Chicago, IL
1896	Aquarium	New York Aquarium, New York, NY
1902	Movie Theater	Electric Theater, Los Angeles, CA
1909	Baseball stadium	Forbes Field, Pittsburgh, PA
1914	Subway	Green Line, Boston, MA
1935	Parking meter	Oklahoma City, OK
1953	Public TV station	KUHT, Houston, TX

Answer these questions about the time line.

1. When was the first hospital opened? _____

2. How many years later was the first public museum opened? _____

3. What was name of the first college? _____

4. What two firsts occurred in Chicago? _____

5. How many years earlier did the Boston Latin public school open than Harvard College? _____

6. What two events occurred in the first decade of the nineteenth century? _____

7. What three events occurred in Philadelphia during the eighteenth century? _____

8. Which occurred earlier— the opening of the first subway or the opening of the first movie

   theater? _____

9. What was the name of the first baseball stadium? _____

10. Now, create a vertical time line to show the following information about modern transportation history.
    - 1869   Transcontinental railroad completed.
    - 1903   Wright brothers fly first powered airplane.
    - 1839   First bicycle powered by pedals.
    - 1908   Henry Ford builds Model T.
    - 1976   First supersonic passenger jet.
    - 1914   Panama Canal opens.
    - 1869   Suez Canal opens.
    - 1963   London subway opens.
    - 1969   U.S. astronauts land on the moon.
    - 1807   Robert Fulton patents the steam boat.
    - 1939   First jet plane invented.
    - 1964   "Bullet train" service begins in Japan.
    - 1873   Cable car system begins in San Francisco.

Create your time line here.

Diagram

2-8

A **diagram** is a drawing that shows the parts of an object or thing. The important parts of the object or thing are labeled.

Look at the diagram of a hot air balloon.

Hot Air Balloon

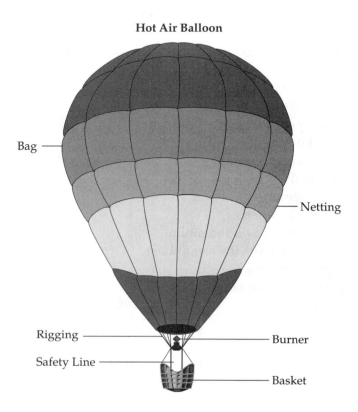

Bag

Netting

Rigging

Burner

Safety Line

Basket

Look at the diagram of a passenger liner. The prow is at the front of the passenger liner.

Passenger Liner

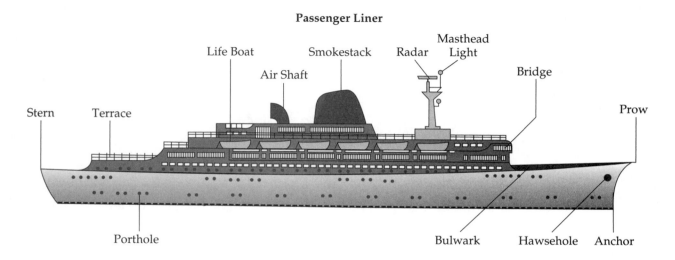

Life Boat

Air Shaft

Smokestack

Radar

Masthead Light

Bridge

Stern

Terrace

Prow

Porthole

Bulwark

Hawsehole

Anchor

38

Copyright © 2010 by Pearson Education, Inc.

Answer these questions about the diagram of the passenger liner.

1. Which is larger—the air shaft or the smokestack? _____

2. Is the radar in front of or behind the bridge? _____

3. Where will you find the stern? _____

4. Is there more than one porthole? _____

5. Where is the anchor? _____

6. What is the highest part of the liner? _____

7. Does the diagram show cables and chains? _____

Use what you know about passenger liners to answer the next three questions.

8. Who do you think you might find on the bridge? _____

9. When do you think a lifeboat might be used? _____

10. When do you think the anchor is dropped? _____

11. Look at the following drawing of a four-door car. Label each of the parts that are listed. You can add and label additional parts.

- Hubcap
- Front bumper
- Front license plate
- Windshield
- Turn signal
- Headlight
- Grill
- Hood
- Door handle
- Side view mirror
- Door
- Tire
- Sunroof
- Trunk

There are many different types of maps. You will most often use a **political map.** A political map shows boundaries of countries, states, or territories along with their major cities. Often, a political map includes a *map scale* to show the relationship between distance on the map and the actual distance on the surface of the earth. A political map will also typically include a compass to show directions on the map.

Look at the political map of Texas that follows. All states and bodies of water that border Texas are shown. The map also shows a country that borders Texas. Further, the map shows the most highly populated cities in Texas. The larger the dot and print size for a city, the larger the population of the city. The dot for the capital city is circled.

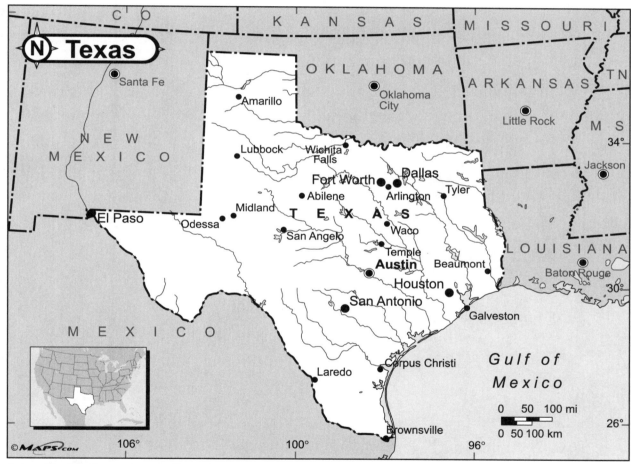

Source: Used with permission of MAPS.com.

Use the map of Texas to answer these questions.

1. Which two large cities are very close to each other? _____

2. Do more people live in Temple than in Odessa? _____

3. What is the capital of Texas? _____

4. How many states border Texas? _____

5. What body of water borders Texas? _____

6. What country borders Texas? _____

7. Which large city in Texas is southeast of the capital? _____

8. Which city in Texas shown is the furthest west? _____

9. In which direction would you travel to get from Amarillo to Lubbock? _____

10. In which direction would you travel to get from San Antonio to Tyler? _____

A **map scale** can be used to find distance between two points on a map. Using the map of Texas in **Activity 2-9**, here is how to find the distance in miles between Austin and San Antonio.

> a. Place the edge of a sheet of paper between the dots on the map for Austin and San Antonio.
> b. Without moving the paper, make a mark on the paper by the dot for Austin. Label this mark as Point 1.
> c. Without moving the paper, make a mark on the paper by the dot for San Antonio. Label this mark as Point 2.
> d. Lay the paper along the miles portion of the map scale to find the distance between Point 1 and Point 2. You will find that the distance between Austin and San Antonio is approximately 90 miles.

If you wanted to find the distance between Lubbock and Odessa in miles using the map in **Activity 2-9**, you would have a problem. The map scale only goes up to 100 miles, but the distance between Lubbock and Odessa is more than 100 miles. Here are the steps you would have to follow in this case.

> a. Place the edge of a sheet of paper between the dots on the map for Lubbock and Odessa.
> b. Without moving the paper, make a mark on the paper by the dot for Lubbock. Label this mark as Point 1.
> c. Without moving the paper, make a mark on the paper by the dot for Odessa. Label this mark as Point 2.
> d. Lay the paper along the miles portion of the map scale to find the distance between the two points. You will find that the distance between Lubbock and Odessa is greater than the length of the scale. This means that the distance between the two cities is more than 100 miles.
> e. Make a mark on the paper by the end of the scale. Label this mark as Point 3.
> f. Move the paper so that Point 3 is at the beginning of the scale. Find the distance between Point 3 and Point 2. This distance is approximately 35 miles.
> g. By adding 35 miles to 100 miles you will find that the distance between Lubbock and Odessa is approximately 135 miles.
>
> Note: Depending on the distance between two cities, you might have to repeat steps f and g one or more times, labeling your marks as Point 4, Point 5, and so on.

Use the map of Texas in Activity 2-9 to answer the following questions.

1. Approximately how far is it in miles from Waco to Temple? _____

2. Approximately how far is it in kilometers from Midland to Odessa? _____

3. Approximately how far is it in miles from El Paso to Santa Fe, New Mexico? _____

4. Approximately how far is it in miles going east from Austin to the border of Louisiana? _____

5. Is the distance between San Antonio and San Angelo more than 250 kilometers? _____

6. Approximately how many miles is Odessa from Mexico if you traveled south? _____

7. Which two cities are closer—Amarillo and Lubbock or San Angelo and Temple? _____

8. If someone drove without stopping at an average speed of 60 mph, about how long would it take them to drive from Austin to San Antonio? _____

Check Yourself Out

Use what you have learned in this unit to answer these questions.

1. What type of graph is best suited for showing information over a period of time? _____

    _____

2. What is another name for a pie graph? _____

    _____

3. When should you use a horizontal bar graph instead of a vertical bar graph? _____

    _____

4. What shows direction on a map? _____

    _____

5. What illustrates the dates of important events over a period of time? _____

    _____

6. What shows a lot of information in a condensed space? _____

    _____

7. What is shown by a political map? _____

    _____

8. Which is a longer distance—50 miles or 50 kilometers? _____

    _____

9. What type of graph uses pictures or drawings to show information? _____

    _____

10. What shows distance on a map? _____

    _____

11. Where is the earliest event shown on a vertical time line? _____

    _____

12. Where is the most recent event shown on a horizontal time line? _____

    _____

Reading and Taking Notes from Textbooks

ACTIVITIES

Learning About the PQRW Strategy: The Preview Step

PQRW is a four-step strategy for reading and taking notes from textbook chapters. Using PQRW will help you to understand the information in your textbooks and produce an accurate and complete set of written notes.

The four steps are:

> **P = Preview**
> **Q = Question**
> **R = Read**
> **W = Write**

The purpose of the **preview** step is to get a quick idea of what the chapter is about. Here is what to do.

- Read the *title*. The title is found at the beginning of the chapter. It is a general descriptive heading that provides an overall sense of what the chapter is about.
- Read the *introduction*. The introduction is the first section of text in the chapter. It is usually one or two paragraphs in length. The introduction alerts you as to what to expect to find in the chapter. Often there is no heading for the introduction.
- Read all the *headings*. Headings break the chapter into sections. They tell you how the information in the chapter is organized. Examine any illustrations and visual aids such as tables and graphs. Read their labels and captions.
- Read the *summary* or *conclusion*. A *summary* restates the main points made in the chapter. A *conclusion* provides a generalization made from the facts and ideas presented in the chapter. If there is a summary or conclusion, you will find it in the last paragraph or two of the chapter. Often there is no heading for the summary or conclusion.

Preview the following shortened chapter about birds from a science textbook titled *Nature All Around Us*. Then answer the questions that follow.

BIRDS

A bird is an animal with feathers and wings. While there are other animals that have wings, only birds have feathers. Birds are vertebrates. This means they have a spinal column or backbone. This also means they are warm-blooded and develop in eggs outside the mother's body. Birds are found all over the world, in every kind of habitat or place where things live. Like people, most birds are active during daylight hours. Also like people, birds rely more on vision and hearing than smell. In this chapter you will learn why birds have always fascinated people.

TYPES OF BIRDS

There are close to 10,000 species of birds in the world. Modem taxonomists, scientists who categorize living things, rely upon DNA to identify the relationships among the different species. DNA is the hereditary material found in the cells of humans and other living things. Closely related birds have more similar DNA than do groups of birds that are distantly related.

The lifestyles of different types of birds are another way to categorize birds. Taxonomists look for birds that live in similar environments or obtain food in similar ways. Here are types of birds that have been categorized in this way.

Water Birds

Water birds obtain most or all of their food from the water. They are able to drink seawater and rid themselves of excess salt. Some water birds live over the open ocean far off from land. Others live close to land. Some live in freshwater lakes and marshes.

Wading Birds

Some birds have very long legs and bills. Their long legs allow them to walk in shallow water to find food. Their long bills allow them to feed below the surface of the water.

Birds of Prey

Birds of prey have hooked beaks, strong claws on their feet, and excellent vision and hearing. They prey on small mammals, fish, and insects as a source of food.

Running Birds

Some birds, such as the ostrich, have a very limited ability to fly. Instead, they rely on their ability to run very fast. Running birds are usually very large and feed primarily on vegetation.

Perching Birds

Perching birds are small birds that can perch or settle on small twigs and branches. The arrangements of their toes and leg tendons allow them to do this. More than half of bird species are perching birds.

BIRDS IN MOVEMENT

Obviously, the primary way birds move is through flight. However, they can also move on land, and some can swim and dive.

In the Air

Birds rely upon lift in order to fly. They produce lift by pushing down on air with their wings. In return, air pushes their wings up. Different wing shapes account for the different flight styles observed in birds. Specialized flight feathers in the wings and tails contribute to lift and minimize resistance as birds fly through the air. Tails are also important for flight. Tail feathers allow birds to change direction and come to a stop when they land.

Figure 1　Birds in Flight

On Land

Most birds can walk and run on land, and some can even climb. Different kinds of birds vary widely in how well they can move on land. Robins can both hop and walk while swifts can only climb. Penguins waddle because their stubby legs are far back from their center of gravity.

In Water

Many birds are excellent swimmers and divers. Most of these birds have webbed toes that act as paddles. These birds use their webbed toes to move themselves under water. Other birds use their wings to move themselves in water. Many birds that catch fish for food can dive to a great depth and remain submerged for a fairly long period of time.

WAYS IN WHICH BIRDS LIVE

Like all animals, birds have to eat, rest, and defend themselves in order to survive. Many birds migrate or move from place to place with the changing seasons of the year as part of their survival mechanism.

Feeding

Birds spend a lot of time searching for food and eating. They cannot store large amounts of food in their bodies because they would not be able to fly given the extra weight. The smaller the bird, the more often it needs to eat. Depending upon the species, birds eat seeds, nectar, fruit, insects, fish, and meat. Some birds are carnivorous, meaning they eat other animals. Some are herbivorous, meaning they eat plants. Still others are omnivorous, meaning they eat almost anything.

Figure 2   A Bird Eating Nectar

Resting

Birds need far less sleep than humans. Like humans, birds sleep to relax their muscles and conserve or save energy. Unlike humans, they do not sleep to refresh their brains. Because most birds are active during the day, they sleep at night. Some birds stand while they sleep. Some sleep perched on a branch, often using only one foot.

Defense

The excellent vision and hearing of birds is their primary or most important means of defense. When one bird spots a predator, it warns the other birds by calling out an alarm. Some birds rely on using camouflage so that they are difficult for predators who hunt them as food to see them. The ways in which birds blend in with their surrounding environment are very imaginative.

> In summary, a bird is an animal that has both feathers and wings. There are close to 10,000 species of birds in the world. Taxonomists often categorize birds by the way they live. Common types of birds include water birds, wading birds, birds of prey, and perching birds. Birds move through the air, on land, and in the water. They spend a lot of time searching for food and eating. Some birds are carnivorous, others are herbivorous, and still others are omnivorous. Birds require little sleep and like people, usually sleep at night. Their excellent vision and hearing is their primary means of defense, although camouflage is also effective.

1. From reading the title, what is this chapter about?

   _____

   _____

   _____

2. What is the single most important fact you learned from reading the introduction?

   _____

   _____

   _____

3. From reading the introduction, what do you expect to learn in this chapter?

   _____

   _____

   _____

4. What are the three major sections of this chapter?

   _____

   _____

   _____

5. What are three facts you learned from reading the summary?

   _____

   _____

   _____

6. List any words whose meanings you learned from reading the chapter.

_____   _____

_____   _____

_____   _____

_____   _____

_____   _____

Question is the second step in PQRW. Questions provide you with a specific purpose for reading a chapter in a textbook. Use the words *who, what, where, why, when,* or *how* to change the first heading into a question. If the heading is already in the form of a question, use that question. If the heading contains more than one idea, write a question for each idea. Write each question in your notebook, leaving space to write its answer.

Read is the third step in PQRW. Read the information that follows the first heading to find the answer(s) to the question(s) you wrote.

Write is the fourth step in PQRW. In this step, write the answer to each question you wrote in your notebook for the first heading.

Repeat these steps for each heading in the chapter with the exception of Introduction, Summary, and Conclusion.

Complete the question, read, and write steps for the chapter "Birds" in Activity 3-1 using the following question-answer notetaking format. The format is partially completed to help you get started.

Title of Textbook: Nature All Around Us

Title of Chapter: Birds

Heading: Types of Birds

Question: What types of birds are there?

Answer: There are 10,000 species of birds

Heading: Types of Birds

Question: Who categorizes birds?

Answer: Taxonomists

Heading: Types of Birds

Question: How are birds categorized?

Answer: They are categorized by DNA and lifestyle.

Heading: Water Birds

Question: What are water birds?

Answer: Birds that obtain most or all their food from the water.

Heading: Water Birds

Question: Where do water birds live?

Answer: Over the open ocean, close to land, and in freshwater lakes and marshes.

Heading: _____

Question: _____

Answer: _____

Heading: _____

Question: _____

Answer: _____

Heading: _____

Question: _____

Answer: _____

Heading: _____

Question: _____

Answer: _____

Heading: _____

Question: _____

Answer: _____

Heading: _____

Question: _____

Answer: _____

Heading: _____

Question: _____

Answer: _____

Heading: _____

Question: _____

Answer: _____

Heading: _____

Question: _____

Answer: _____

Heading: _____

Question: _____

Answer: _____

Heading: _____

Question: _____

Answer: _____

Heading: _____

Question: _____

Answer: _____

Heading: _____

Question: _____

Answer: _____

Heading: _____

Question: _____

Answer: _____

Heading: _____

Question: _____

Answer: _____

Heading: _____

Question: _____

Answer: _____

Heading: _____

Question: _____

Answer: _____

Heading: _____

Question: _____

Answer: _____

Heading: _____

Question: _____

Answer: _____

Heading: _____

Question: _____

Answer: _____

Heading: _____

Question: _____

Answer: _____

Heading: _____

Question: _____

Answer: _____

Heading: _____

Question: _____

Answer: _____

Complete the question-answer notetaking format that follows this shortened chapter about weather from a science textbook titled *Forces Around Us.*

WEATHER

Weather is the state of the atmosphere or our surrounding environment at a given time and place. When describing weather, we talk about temperature, humidity, cloudiness, precipitation, wind, and pressure. All of these elements are organized into various weather systems. Meteorologists are scientists who study these systems and forecast what the weather will be like in different places.

Temperature

Temperature is a measure of how hot the air is. Meteorologists in the United States use the Fahrenheit scale to describe how hot the air is. This is a scale where 32 degrees is assigned to the temperature where water freezes and 212 degrees to the temperature where water boils. Temperature is highest in the tropics and lowest near the poles. Highest temperatures occur during midafternoon and coldest temperatures around dawn.

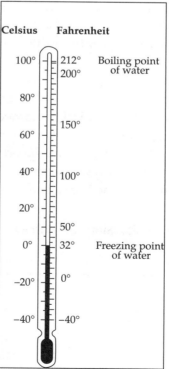

Figure 3   Recording Temperature

Temperature decreases the higher in elevation you go. It is colder in the mountains than at sea level.

Humidity

Humidity is the amount of water vapor in the air. The most common measure of humidity is relative humidity. This is the amount of vapor in the air divided by the air's capacity to hold vapor at whatever the temperature is at the moment. If the amount of water vapor in the air remains the same, the relative humidity decreases as the air is heated and increases as the air is cooled. This is why the relative humidity is usually highest around dawn and lowest in midafternoon. This is the opposite of what is found for the temperature of the air.

Cloudiness

Clouds are produced by the cooling of the air as it rises. A cloud can take any of several different forms. Four types of clouds are cumulus, stratus, cirrus, and nimbus. Fog is a cloud that touches the ground. It typically occurs when the temperature on the surface is much lower than the air directly above it. Visibility is very poor during conditions of thick fog.

Precipitation

Precipitation is moisture that occurs when droplets and crystals in clouds grow large enough to fall to the ground. There are a number of forms of precipitation: rain, drizzle, freezing rain, snow, hail, and sleet.

Wind

Wind is the horizontal movement of air. It is named for the direction from which it comes. A northerly wind comes from the north, a westerly wind from the west, and so on. The average wind speed is from 5–15 mph. The wind speed in hurricanes can be anywhere from 75 mph and higher depending upon the intensity of the hurricane. Hurricanes are classified on

Table 1   Saffir-Simpson Hurricane Scale

Category	Wind Speed (mph)
1	75–95
2	96–110
3	111–130
4	131–155
5	>155

the Saffir-Simpson Scale according to their wind speed (see Table 1). The highest wind speeds of all occur during tornadoes.

Air Pressure

Air pressure is the force of the air on a given surface divided by the area of that surface. It plays an important role in all weather systems. Air pressure decreases the higher you go. The air pressure at the top of a mountain is much less than at sea level. This is why people who are not used to going up into mountains complain of feeling lightheaded.

Large regions in the atmosphere that have higher air pressure than the surrounding regions are called high-pressure areas. Regions with lower air pressure than the surrounding regions are called low- pressure areas. Watch out when air pressure falls rapidly. This usually means a storm is on the way.

Causes of Weather

All weather results from heating from the sun. A region receives more heat when the sun is higher in the sky and there are more hours of sunlight in a day. The high sun of the tropics makes this a very warm area. In the Northern Hemisphere the days are long in the summer. At the same time the Southern Hemisphere is experiencing winter.

Weather Forecasting

The development of computers, satellites, and radar has greatly increased the accuracy of weather forecasts. Meteorologists are now able to provide warning of a major storm as much as a week in advance. However, because weather systems are so variable, they cannot accurately forecast the details of weather beyond two weeks in advance.

Conclusion

Weather is important to all of us in our everyday lives. We plan our activities and the clothing we wear depending upon what we think the weather will be like. Even though weather predictions have become more and more accurate, they remain far from perfect. So be kind to the poor weather

Title of Textbook: _____

Title of Chapter: _____

Heading: _____

Question: _____

Answer: _____

Heading: _____

Question: _____

Answer: _____

Heading: _____

Question: _____

Answer: _____

Heading: _____

Question: _____

Answer: _____

Heading: _____

Question: _____

Answer: _____

Heading: _____

Question: _____

Answer: _____

Heading: _____

Question: _____

Answer: _____

Heading: _____

Question: _____

Answer: _____

Heading: _____

Question: _____

Answer: _____

Heading: _____

Question: _____

Answer: _____

Heading: _____

Question: _____

Answer: _____

Heading: _____

Question: _____

Answer: _____

Heading: _____

Question: _____

Answer: _____

Heading: _____

Question: _____

Answer: _____

Heading: _____

Question: _____

Answer: _____

Heading: _____

Question: _____

Answer: _____

Heading: _____

Question: _____

Answer: _____

Heading: _____

Question: _____

Answer: _____

Heading: _____

Question: _____

Answer: _____

Answer the questions that follow to be sure you understand the PQRW strategy.

1. Write the name of each step:

   P = _____

   Q = _____

   R = _____

   W = _____

2. What can you learn from the introduction to a chapter?

   _____

   _____

3. What is the purpose of headings?

   _____

   _____

4. What is the difference between a summary and a conclusion?

   _____

   _____

5. Why is it important to form questions?

   _____

   _____

6. What words are used to change headings into questions?

   _____

   _____

7. What should you do if a heading contains more than one idea?

   _____

   _____

Using PQRW on Your Own

Use PQRW with a chapter from one of your own textbooks

Title of Textbook: _____

Title of Chapter: _____

Heading: _____

Question: _____

Answer: _____

Heading: _____

Question: _____

Answer: _____

Heading: _____

Question: _____

Answer: _____

Heading: _____

Question: _____

Answer: _____

Heading: _____

Question: _____

Answer: _____

Heading: _____

Question: _____

Answer: _____

Heading: _____

Question: _____

Answer: _____

Heading: _____

Question: _____

Answer: _____

Heading: _____

Question: _____

Answer: _____

Heading: _____

Question: _____

Answer: _____

Heading: _____

Question: _____

Answer: _____

Heading: _____

Question: _____

Answer: _____

Heading: _____

Question: _____

Answer: _____

Heading: _____

Question: _____

Answer: _____

Heading: _____

Question: _____

Answer: _____

Heading: _____

Question: _____

Answer: _____

Taking Notes in Class

ACTIVITIES

Your teachers will often present information on some subject by talking about it. This is known as a *lecture*. When one of your teachers presents a lecture, you will need to take written notes. Note-taking becomes an increasingly important skill as you progress through school.

There are three stages of **notetaking**. The **first stage** includes things to do **before** you come to class. The **second stage** includes things to do **during** class. The **third stage** includes things to do **after** class.

Look at the checklist that follows. It shows the things you should do for each stage of notetaking. Place a checkmark ✓ next to each thing you do most or all the time.

Get Ready Stage (First Stage)

_____ I have my notetaking materials ready.

_____ I review my notes from the previous class session.

_____ I complete all my reading assignments.

Take Notes Stage (Second Stage)

_____ I listen for signal words and statements that tell me that something is important to write in my notes.

_____ I write using abbreviations and symbols.

_____ I write using the fewest words possible.

_____ I copy information the teacher writes on the chalkboard.

_____ I circle words I write but whose meanings I do not know.

_____ I place a "?" next to anything I write but do not understand.

After Notes Stage (Third Stage)

_____ I ask my teacher or use my textbook and reference books to clarify anything I wrote but did not understand.

_____ I compare my notes with those of other students.

_____ I use the glossary in my textbook or a dictionary to learn the meanings of unknown words.

_____ I rewrite my notes to make them as legible, complete, and accurate as possible.

Your teachers will often use **signal words** to alert you that what they just said is important to write in your notes. By identifying signal words, you will be more likely to write important information in your notes.

Here are some signal words teachers often use:

moreover	furthermore	similarly	however
conversely	then	before	after
next	therefore	thus	finally
hence	though	since	consequently

Read the following shortened lecture about caves given by a teacher. Some of the signal words from the box above are used in the lecture. Circle each signal word used in the lecture as you read it. The same signal word may be used more than once.

CAVES

Caves are holes in the ground, usually hollowed out by water. Rainwater trickles down through the ground; consequently, the minerals in the rocks are dissolved. Therefore, hollows and tunnels are formed. Some caves are very long passages, though other caves are huge open spaces. You will find stalactites hanging down from the roofs of caves. They look like icicles. Conversely, stalagmites grow up from the floors of caves. Though caves have no light, many animals live in caves. Many are blind. Thus they depend on smell, touch, or echoes to find their way. Bats, especially, prefer to live in caves. Other cave animals include birds and fish. Therefore, caves play an important part in sustaining life.

Your teachers will also use **signal statements** to alert you that what they just said is important to write in your notes.

Here are some signal statements teachers often use:

remember that	above all	the basic concept
a primary concern	a significant factor	a major event
should be noted	the chief outcome	most of all
a central issue	of course	it all boils down to
on the other hand	in the meantime	don't forget

Read the following shortened lecture about animal communication given by a teacher. Some of the signal statements from the box above are used in the lecture. Circle each signal statement used as you read. The same signal statement may be used more than once.

ANIMAL COMMUNICATION

Communication means to pass on messages and information. It should be noted that animals use sound, sight, and movement to communicate. Also, it should be noted they use scent, taste, touch, and electrical signals to communicate.

A central issue in studying animal behavior is the extent to which they can think. The examples that follow demonstrate they certainly can. Some animals puff themselves up to make themselves appear bigger than they really are. Of course, this makes other animals think twice about attacking them. Wolves communicate with body language. Their ability to communicate with each other is a significant factor in their survival. Still, wolves are a threatened animal. This is a primary concern of many environmentalists. Of course, some people such as ranchers would be happy to see wolves disappear.

There are many other kinds of animal communication. It all boils down to which animal and the purpose for their communication. The basic concept here is that just like humans, animals express themselves.

Your teacher will talk faster than you can write. It is important to be able to write notes quickly to keep up. A good way to do this is to **abbreviate words** as you write your notes. To abbreviate a word is to write it in shortened form.

Here are commonly used abbreviations. Write the full word next to each abbreviation.

1. pt _____

2. cu _____

3. Aug _____

4. sgt _____

5. sq _____

6. pl _____

7. qt _____

8. rev _____

9. mt _____

10. pseudo _____

11. sr _____

12. gal _____

13. capt _____

14. inc _____

15. kg _____

16. lat _____

17. est _____

18. dept _____

19. dist _____

20. lib _____

Forming Abbreviations

You can form your own abbreviations for words as you take notes. Keep in mind that you must be able to later identify the entire word from an abbreviation you write.

Here are three ways to abbreviate words. Examples are provided for each way. When you abbreviate a word while taking notes in class, choose the way that works best for that word.

Write only the beginning of the word.

Word	Abbreviation
executive	exec
recipe	rec
suggestion	sugg
medicine	med

Leave out the vowels (do not use this way if the word begins with a vowel).

Word	Abbreviation
hemisphere	hmsphr
present	prsnt
government	gvrnmnt
savage	svg

For words with one syllable, write just the first and last letter.

Word	Abbreviation
word	wd
down	dn
slight	st
cart	ct

Abbreviate each of the following words. For each word, use the way that works best for you.

1. parenthesis _____

2. reside _____

3. born _____

4. incubator _____

5. catch _____

6. peninsula _____

7. fancy _____

8. gobble _____

9. senate _____

10. modest _____

11. gauze _____

12. luxury _____

13. referee _____

14. brunette _____

15. road _____

16. stethoscope _____

17. encounter _____

18. literature _____

19. blob _____

20. episode _____

Using Symbols

Another way to increase your notetaking speed is to use **symbols** in place of words or terms. Here are some common words and terms and the symbols used in their place.

%	percent	&	and	+	plus
@	at	#	number	$	money
=	equals, equal to	?	question	−	minus
×	multiply	∠	angle	∞	infinity
÷	divided by	≠	not equal to	\	difference
>	greater than	<	less than	‖	parallel
⊥	perpendicular	∴	therefore	°	degree
′	minute	″	second	¢	cent

Rewrite each sentence using abbreviations and symbols as appropriate. You should be able to understand your rewritten sentence at a later time.

1. The question the United Nations is most concerned with is how to make certain that money given to one poor country for development is not greater than that given to another country.

   _____

   _____

2. Robert finished the race in the fast time of 16 minutes, 10 seconds because the track had only one sharp angle turn.

   _____

   _____

3. The difference between parallel lines and perpendicular lines is that parallel lines go in the same direction, whereas perpendicular lines form right angles.

   _____

   _____

4. I thought that 20 percent of 80 is less than 10, but it is actually greater than 10.

   _____

   _____

5. I am short on money; therefore, I am not going to see the movie.

   _____

   _____

Another way to increase your notetaking speed is to write short sentences that contain the fewest words necessary to capture important information. For example, instead of writing, "Asia is the world's largest continent, both in land area and the number of people living there," you could write, "Asia has the most people and land of any continent." This reduces the number of words in the sentence from 17 to 10.

Rewrite each of the following sentences using the fewest words necessary to capture the important information.

1. Photosynthesis is a very remarkable process used by green plants in which each green plant takes in or absorbs energy from the sun and uses the energy to combine carbon dioxide from the air with water to make food that is sugary.

   _____

   _____

2. An epic is an adventure story that is written in the form of a long poem that follows the great deeds of human heroes as they struggle against various dangers that have a magical quality.

   _____

   _____

3. The space shuttle is a craft that can be used many more times than once and has the capability to land on a runway on one mission, and then blast off once again on another mission to some other place in space.

   _____

   _____

4. Lizards cannot control or manage the heat of their own body, and so they rely heavily on the rays from the sun for warmth.

   _____

   _____

5. Scorpions are creatures that are most active at night and are found in tropical and warm temperate regions in a wide range of habitats that can be anything from deserts such as those found in Asia to rainforests such as those found in South America.

   _____

   _____

A Two-Column Notetaking Format

When presenting a lecture, your teacher will identify the *topic* of the lecture. The topic is the subject matter of the lecture. Your teacher will present one or more *main ideas* about the topic. A main idea is an important point about the topic. Each main idea will have one or more *supporting details*. A supporting detail can be a fact, personal experience, example, description, or anything that provides more detail about a main idea.

Use the following two-column format for taking notes in class to help you record the important information your teacher presents about a topic.

Class_____   Date_____   Page Number_____

Topic _____

Main Ideas	Supporting Details
Questions	
Vocabulary	

Here is what to do when taking notes in class using this two-column notetaking format:

- Record the date of the class session and the name of the class.
- Record the topic of the lecture once your teacher reveals it.
- Each time your teacher provides a main idea, write it in the Main Idea column. It is helpful to number each main idea beginning with 1.
- Next to each main idea, write in the Supporting Details column any supporting details your teacher provides about the main idea. Again, it is helpful to number each supporting detail.
- Leave space between a main idea and its details and the next main idea and its details. Doing this makes it easier to study your notes and add additional notes later as needed.
- Place a "?" next to anything you write but do not understand. Write what you do not understand as a question in the Questions section of the notetaking format.

74

- Any time your teacher uses a word whose meaning you do not know, write that word in the Vocabulary section of the notetaking format.
- Write using abbreviations, symbols, and short sentences or statements.
- Don't be too concerned about punctuation; being too concerned can slow you down.
- Use only one side of the paper. In this way you can lay your notes side by side when you study them for a test.
- Use as many sheets of paper as needed. Be sure to number each.

Answer these questions to check your understanding.

1. What is a topic? _____

2. What is a main idea? _____

3. What is a supporting detail? _____

4. Why is it a good idea to write your notes only on one side of the paper?

   _____

   _____

5. What should you do when you write a word whose meaning you do not know?

   _____

   _____

First notes are the notes you take while in class. Because you have to take notes quickly in class, your first notes may be somewhat illegible and difficult to read. They may not be complete. They may contain abbreviations and symbols. They may contain questions to be answered and words whose meanings need to be learned.

Read the first notes a student took in a science class from a lecture about the heart and blood.

Class _____ Science _____ **Date** _4/12_ _____ **Page Number** _1_

Topic The Heart and Blood _____

Main Idea	Supporting Details
1. Blood circulates arnd bdy	1. Reddish lqd 2. Carries food and oxy 2 bdy cells? 3. removes waste
2. Heart pumps bld arnd bdy	1. Has 2 pumps 2. 1 snds bld 2 lungs 2 collect oxy & bld returns to hrt 3. othr pump sends bld 2 rest of bdy
3. Bld has 2 main types of cells	1. White protects bdy agnst dis 2. red sends oxy frm lungs 2 rest of bdy 3. red contains hemoglobin
4. How much bld in bdy?	1. depends on bdy size 2. adlt 176 lb has 1.3 gal 3. child 88 lb has $^1/_2$ that

Questions
What kind of waste does blood remove?
Vocabulary
circulates
hemoglobin

Use these first notes to answer the following questions:

1. What is the lecture about?

   _____

2. How many main ideas are there?

   _____

3. What are the two main types of cells found in blood?

   _____

4. Which type of cell protects the body against disease?

   _____

5. What was the student who took the notes not sure about?

   _____

6. What does the amount of blood depend on?

   _____

7. What words did the student write but not know the meaning of?

   _____

8. What abbreviations were used by the student?

   _____

9. What two symbols were used by the student?

   _____

10. How many pumps does the heart have?

   _____

Rewritten Notes

Rewritten notes are a revision of your first notes. Here are the things to do to rewrite your first notes.

- Write the entire word for each abbreviation.
- Change each symbol into the word it represents.
- Expand short sentences and statements into full sentences.
- Ask your teacher or use your textbooks or reference books to answer any questions you wrote in the Questions section. Add what you learn to your notes.
- Use the glossary of your textbook or a dictionary to learn and write the meanings of any words you wrote in the Vocabulary section.
- Check with other students to make sure you didn't miss important things your teacher said. Add any information needed.

Here are rewritten notes from the first notes from Activity **4-9**.

| Class | Science | Date | 4/12 | Page Number | 1 |

Topic The Heart and Blood

Main Idea	Supporting Details
1. Blood circulates around the body.	1. It is a reddish liquid. 2. Blood carries food and oxygen to the cells in the body. 3. Blood takes away waste and unwanted materials including carbon dioxide, which is breathed out.
2. The heart pumps blood around the body.	1. It is divided into two pumps. 2. One pump sends blood to the lungs to collect oxygen. 3. When blood returns to the heart, the other pump sends it to the rest of the body.
3. Blood has two main types of cells.	1. White blood cells protect the body against diseases. 2. Red blood cells send oxygen from lungs to the tissues of the body through the blood. 3. Red blood cells contain hemoglobin.
4. How much blood does the body contain?	1. It depends on the size of one's body. 2. An adult who weighs 176 pounds has about 1.3 gallons of blood. 3. A child who weighs 88 pounds has half the blood of an adult who weighs 176 pounds.

Questions
What kind of waste does blood remove? Carbon dioxide, which is breathed out.

Vocabulary
Circulates — Moves about or flows freely.
Hemoglobin — An iron-containing protein in the red blood cells. It carries oxygen from the lungs to the tissues of the body and carries carbon dioxide from the tissues to the lungs.

Answer these questions by using the first notes and the rewritten notes.

1. What detail was added to the main idea that blood circulates around the body?

   _____

2. What is hemoglobin?

   _____

3. What is one type of waste material removed by blood?

   _____

4. What is the third main idea?

   _____

5. About how many gallons of blood does a child weighing 88 pounds have?

   _____

6. How is carbon dioxide removed from the body?

   _____

7. What are three types of blood vessels?

   _____

8. What does circulate mean?

   _____

Read the following shortened lecture given in a social studies class.

> By about 1430, Europeans were building new types of ships that could sail through rough weather and carry enough food and drink for long voyages. Merchants throughout Europe wanted to find routes to rich countries such as India, China, and the Spice Islands. They hoped to make a lot of money by trading with these countries. Sailors were sent to find routes across the seas. Sometimes they were successful; other times they accidently found different countries. In 1492 Christopher Columbus sailed across the ocean. He hoped to find China but found the Americas instead. The Spanish began settling in the Americas in the 1500s. They built many large cities. During the years 1519–1522, Ferdinand Magellan became the first navigator to sail across the Pacific. He was killed in the Philippines. However, his crew and ship went on to complete the first round-the-world voyage.

Examine the following first notes a student wrote from the lecture.

Class ___Social Studies___   **Date** ___3/23___   **Page Number** _1_

Topic _Age of Explorers_

Main Idea	Supporting Details
1. Europeans blt new types of ships	1. arnd 1430 2. cld sail thru bad wthr 3. engh fd & drnk 4 lng voy? 4. caravel pop ship
2. Lkd 4 rts 2 India, China, & Spice Isl 3. Sailors sent 2 fnd rts cross seas 4. Chris Columbus 5. Spanish sttld in amer 6. Ferdinand Magellan	1. wntd $ by trdng 1. sometimes fnd new countrs 1. 1492 sld crss atlan 1. 1500s 2. Wnt to rch China but fnd Americas 1. 1519–1522 2. 1st nav 2 sail crss Pac 3. klld in Philippines 4. crew & ship went on 2 complt 1st rnd wrld voy

Questions
Why was a caravel a popular ship?

Vocabulary
voyage
route
navigator

Use the two-column notetaking format that follows to rewrite the first notes.

Class_____ **Date**_____ **Page Number**_____

Topic _____

Main Ideas	Supporting Details

Questions

Vocabulary

Using Reference Sources

Reference sources are used to find background information, to locate facts, and to answer questions. Look at the graphic organizer. It shows the major types of reference sources. Then read the brief description of each type of reference source.

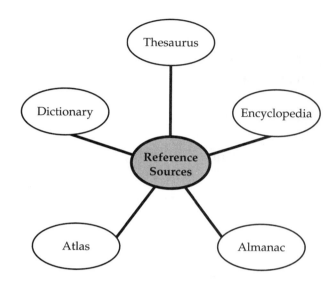

A **dictionary** provides information about the meanings, pronunciation, and spelling of words.

A **thesaurus** contains synonyms for words. A *synonym* is a word that has the same or nearly the same meaning of another word. A thesaurus may contain antonyms for words. An *antonym* is a word that has the opposite meaning on another word.

An **encyclopedia** contains articles and information on a variety of subjects.

An **almanac** contains very specific facts and data on a variety of subjects.

An **atlas** is a collection of maps.

Write the type of the reference source you would use to

1. Find the name of the third-longest suspension bridge in the world. _____

2. Find a similar word to use instead of "beautiful." _____

3. Learn about the water cycle. _____

4. Locate which countries border France. _____

5. Learn about the childhood of George Washington. _____

6. Learn the two most common meanings of "liberty." _____

7. Learn as much as you can about the original 13 American colonies. _____

8. Learn how to pronounce "iguana." _____

A **format** is the way information is packaged. Reference sources may be in a *print* format or in an *electronic* format.

PRINT FORMAT

A **print format** uses paper. Each reference source is presented in the form of a book. Here is a print format example of each of the reference sources you learned about in Activity **5-1**.

> *Dictionary:* The American Heritage Dictionary of the English Language
> *Thesaurus:* Webster's New World Thesaurus
> *Encyclopedia:* Encyclopedia Britannica
> *Almanac:* World Almanac
> *Atlas:* National Geographic Atlas of the World

Using your school or public library, locate and write the title of a print format example of each of the following.

1. Encyclopedia _____

2. Dictionary _____

3. Atlas _____

4. Almanac _____

5. Atlas _____

ELECTRONIC FORMAT

An **electronic format** is any format other than print. The most important electronic formats you should use are the Internet and CD-ROMs.

The Internet is a worldwide network that allows you to connect to millions of computers using your own computer. The World Wide Web is one part of the Internet. It contains information presented on Web sites. Search engines such as Google and Yahoo allow you to locate Web sites.

A **CD-ROM** is a thin disk that can store thousands of pages of information. You can retrieve and print the information using a computer. You cannot add to or change the information in any way.

6. Locate an Internet Web site that provides information about presidents of the United States. Write the Web site address (also known as a URL). You will find the address of the Web site at the top left portion of the computer screen. It will begin with http:_____

_____

7. What is a limitation of a CD-ROM reference source?

_____

_____

Learning about a Dictionary

A **dictionary,** whether in print format or electronic format, provides information about words.

PRINT FORMAT DICTIONARY

Each page of a print format dictionary contains a number of *entry words*. Entry words are the words about which information is presented. They are printed in bold type to make them easy to locate.

At the top of each page are two *guide words*. The first guide word is called the *opening guide word*. It shows the first entry word on the page. The second guide word is called the *closing guide word*. It shows the last entry word on the page. The guide words help you locate a word quickly.

Here is the information you will find about entry words in most dictionaries.

a. *Meaning or meanings:* Many entry words have more than one meaning. If so, the meanings are numbered to show how commonly they are used. The most commonly used meaning is listed as 1, the next most common meaning as 2, and so on.

b. *Syllabication:* The entry word is shown broken into syllables. If no syllabication is shown, the entry word has just one syllable.

c. *Phonetic respelling:* The entry word is shown in phonetic respelling form, usually in parentheses ( ). The phonetic respelling helps the user pronounce the entry word.

d. *Usage:* Sometimes one or more sentences containing the entry word is provided to show how the word might be used.

e. *Parts of speech:* The parts of speech of the entry word are shown. Some entry words have just one part of speech. An abbreviation is typically used to represent a part of speech as follows:

noun (n)	verb (v)	adjective (adj)	conjunction (con)
pronoun (pron)	adverb (adv)	preposition (prep)	

f. *Variants:* Different forms of the entry word are shown. For example, *directed, directing,* and *directs* may be shown for the entry word *direct*.

g. *Etymology:* Sometimes information is provided about the history of an entry word from its beginning to its present form. The language the entry word came from may be noted as well as any changes in its spelling or meaning.

h. *Synonym and/or antonym:* A synonym and/or an antonym may be shown for the entry word. A synonym (syn) is a word that has the same or nearly the same meaning as another word. An antonym (ant) is a word that has the opposite meaning of another word.

i. *Illustration:* A drawing or picture of the entry word may be provided.

j. *Pronunciation keys:* A *short pronunciation key* is provided at the bottom of each right-hand page of the dictionary. The short pronunciation key shows the special symbols and spellings that are used to show sounds when pronouncing a word. A *long pronunciation key* is located at the front of the dictionary. The long pronunciation key shows the different sounds of the English language and the different ways these sounds are spelled.

1. Look at the following entry from a page from a print format dictionary. In each box, write the letter that represents the underlined information in the entry. Refer to the descriptions of the information found about entry words at the beginning of this activity as you do this. For example, use the letter "c" to show where the phonetic respelling of dispute appears in the entry.

dis–pute   (dĭ–spyōōt′)   v.   1. To argue against; disagree with.

They *disputed* your claim that you were the smartest kid in your class.

2. To argue or fight over.   syn. squabble; ant. agree   n.   An argument or quarrel.

syn. disagreement.   From Old French *disputer*.   **disputed, disputing, disputes.**

ELECTRONIC FORMAT DICTIONARY

Dictionaries are also available on the Internet. Most are free. Some have additional features that can be purchased. Dictionaries can also be purchased as a CD-ROM or as a download from the Internet to an iPod.

A good example of a dictionary on the Internet is the Merriam-Webster Online Dictionary. The address of this site is: http://www.m-w.com/. Go to this site to see the information provided about the entry word *dispute*.

2. What valuable feature is provided at this site that is not provided in most print format dictionaries?

_____

Use a print format and/or an electronic format dictionary to answer the following questions.

1. What is the most common meaning of **hazel** as a noun?

    _____

2. What is the phonetic respelling of **distinguish**? _____

3. What is the etymology of **overture**?

    _____

    _____

4. What parts of speech are shown for **savage**?

    _____   _____

    _____   _____

5. What is the most common meaning of **grade** as verb?

    _____

6. What part of speech is **impetuous**? _____

7. What is an antonym for **relaxed**? _____

8. Is **gale** a noun or a verb? _____

9. How many syllables does **photosynthesis** contain? _____

10. What variants are shown for **shuttle**?

    _____   _____

    _____   _____

11. Does **inquisitive** mean to be afraid? _____ If not, what does it mean?

    _____

12. What are three meanings of **offense**?

    _____

    _____

    _____

Using a Thesaurus

A **thesaurus** contains synonyms for words. A *synonym* is a word that has the same or nearly the same meaning as another word. When using a thesaurus, you will usually find more than one synonym for a word. In this case, you will need to select the synonym that best fits the context in which you wish to use the synonym.

A thesaurus may also include antonyms. An *antonym* is a word that has the opposite meaning of another word. However, you will primarily use a thesaurus to locate synonyms. Using a thesaurus can increase your vocabulary and add precision and variety to your writing.

A *print format* thesaurus is generally found in two forms.

- In *dictionary form*, entry words are listed in alphabetical order. All synonyms for the word are found on the page where the word appears.
- In *index form*, entry words are classified by categories. An index in the back of the thesaurus guides you to the page or pages where the word appears.

You can also find a thesaurus in an *electronic format* on the Internet or on a CD-ROM. For example, *Roget II: The New Thesaurus* can be found at the following Internet address: http://education. yahoo.com/reference/thesaurus/.

Use a print format and/or electronic thesaurus to find a synonym for each of the following words. The context in which the synonym is to be used is shown in the parentheses ( ).

1. innocent (used as an adjective for someone who does not have much worldly experience)

_____

2. probability (used as a noun to suggest a probable event or condition)

_____

3. incline (used as a verb to suggest bending in a certain way)

_____

4. elaborate (used as a verb to suggest explaining something more fully)

_____

5. colleague (used as a noun to refer to someone who shares the same profession or work)

_____

6. emphasis (used as a noun to suggest special importance given to something)

_____

7. fundamental (used as an adjective to suggest serving as a foundation)

   _____

8. outrageous (used as an adjective to suggest an act that is offensive or wrong)

   _____

9. sarcastic (used as an adjective to suggest something expressing or characterized by sarcasm)

   _____

10. contradict (used as a verb to suggest or assert the opposite of something)

   _____

Choosing the Best Synonym

When using a thesaurus, you will typically find more than one synonym for a word. Choose the synonym that best fits your purpose. You may need to use a dictionary to learn the meanings and usage of some of the synonyms shown.

For example, for the word *lengthen*, you will find the synonyms *extend* and *prolong*. Both of these synonyms mean to make longer, but *prolong* refers to time, such as when someone prolongs a vacation. "*I have to extend the ladder to reach the light fixture*" makes sense. "*I have to prolong the ladder to reach the light fixture*" does not make sense because *prolong* is not being used in the context of the sentence.

For each of the following sentences, choose the synonym that best replaces the highlighted word. Write that synonym on the blank line.

1. The accident was the **result** of carelessness. (conclusion, consequence, end)

   _____

2. I wanted to go to the movies, but I **only** had two dollars. (barely, just, merely)

   _____

3. Tommy hid his baseball card collection in a **safe** place. (guarded, protected, secure)

   _____

4. Tanya's performance in the dance recital was **perfect**. (exact, flawless, ideal)

   _____

5. There is only a **minor** chance of rain tomorrow. (slight, trivial)

   _____

6. Maria was **anxious** about her first day in seventh grade. (concerned, upset, worried)

   _____

7. Our long car **journey** across the state took two days. (expedition, tour, trip, voyage)

   _____

8. Tony spent an **excessive** amount of time cleaning his room. (extravagant, lavish, undue)

   _____

9. The **normal** temperature for a person is 98.6 degrees Fahrenheit. (commonplace, everyday, standard)

_____

10. The desk was too **heavy** for me to lift. (massive, stout, weighty)

_____

Using an Encyclopedia

5-7

An **encyclopedia** contains articles on a variety of subjects. Each of the articles is written by one or more experts. A *general encyclopedia* includes overview articles on a wide range of subjects. A *subject encyclopedia* includes very detailed articles covering all aspects of a particular subject such as science or history.

1. Use your school or public library to find a general encyclopedia in *print format*. Write the name of this encyclopedia and the year it was published.

   Name _____

   Year _____

2. Find a subject encyclopedia in *print format*. Write the name of this encyclopedia and the year it was published.

   Name _____

   Year _____

A *print format* encyclopedia may consist of a single volume or a set of volumes. Articles appear in alphabetical order according to subject. For an encyclopedia that includes more than one volume, letters on the spine of each volume (A–B, C–E, and so on) show the first letter of subjects that are included in that volume.

3. Find an encyclopedia in *print format* that consists of one volume. Write the name of this encyclopedia and the year it was published.

   Name _____

   Year _____

4. Find an encyclopedia in *print format* that consists of a set of volumes. Write the name of this encyclopedia and the year it was published.

   Name _____

   Year _____

5. How many volumes does this encyclopedia contain?

   _____

The index of an encyclopedia identifies the pages on which information about a subject appears. For an encyclopedia that is a single volume, the index is found at the end of the volume. For an encyclopedia that consists of a set of volumes, there is usually a separate index volume.

6. What is the purpose of an index?

_____

You can also find an encyclopedia in an *electronic format* on the Internet or on a CD-ROM. Articles contained on a CD-ROM encyclopedia often contain multimedia information such as sound, video, and even animation. Further, you can print the articles. Wikipedia (http://www.wikipedia.org) is a unique encyclopedia on the Internet. Articles are contributed and edited by users of the site.

7. Find an encyclopedia on the Internet. Write the address of the site at which this encyclopedia is found.

_____

Practice Using an Encyclopedia

Use a *print format* or an *electronic format* encyclopedia to answer the following questions about the Constitution of the United States. Write the name of the encyclopedia or its Internet address here.

_____

1. In what year did the Constitution go into effect?_____

2. The Constitution puts forth three separate branches of government. What are they?

_____   _____   _____

3. A preamble is an introductory statement. Write the complete preamble to the Constitution.

_____

_____

_____

_____

_____

_____

_____

_____

4. How many Articles are contained in the Constitution?_____

5. What does Article IV of the Constitution explain?

_____

_____

6. An amendment is a change to a document. What did Amendment VIII outlaw?

_____

7. What right was granted by Amendment XIX?

_____

8. Which amendment declared slavery illegal?_____

9. Is there an amendment that bans the burning of the United States flag?_____

10. Is there an amendment that guarantees every person the right to a speedy trial?_____

An **almanac** contains facts on a large number of subjects. Because an almanac is published each year, you will find up-to-date information presented with many lists, charts, and tables.

A *print format* almanac is a single volume with information arranged according to subject. You can find the information you need using the table of contents and index. An almanac may also be found in *electronic format* on the Internet or a CD-ROM.

Most almanacs are *general almanacs* that provide information about the world, important events, business and the economy, entertainment, sports, and much more. An example is the *World Almanac and Book of Facts*. Some almanacs are *specialized almanacs*. The *Old Farmer's Almanac* has been published since 1792. It emphasizes weather, astronomy, and food and gardening, with much practical advice offered.

Use a *print format* or an *electronic format* almanac to answer the following questions. Write the name of the almanac or its Internet address you use here.

_____

1. In what state is the Valley Forge National Historic Park found?_____

2. What is the height in feet of the Sears Tower located in Chicago?_____

3. In what year did the Liberty Bell reach Philadelphia?_____

4. What is the name of the capital of Estonia?_____

5. What was the former name of the country now named Myanmar?_____

6. Who hit the most home runs in major league baseball in 2002?_____
    How many home runs did he hit that year?_____

7. What are two of the major industries of Colorado?

    _____   _____

8. Where was the actress Jennifer Lopez born? _____
    In what year was she born?_____

9. In what year was Martin Luther King Jr. Day first officially observed?_____

10. Who won the Nobel Peace Prize in 2002?_____

Using an Atlas

An **atlas** is a collection of maps. The most common type of atlas is one that contains *political maps* (a political map shows government boundaries). Another common type of atlas contains *physical maps* (a physical map shows features of the earth's surface). Atlases can be found in both *print formats* and *electronic formats*.

Use one or more political maps to answer the following questions.

1. Which five states are along the Gulf of Mexico?

    _____   _____

    _____   _____

    _____

2. Is Turkey north or south of the Black Sea? _____

3. What large island lies just off the coast of Mozambique? _____

4. Which four countries border Peru?

    _____   _____

    _____   _____

5. Which Asian country has the largest land area? _____

Use physical maps to answer the following questions.

6. Mount Everest is the highest mountain in the world. It lies between the border of which two countries?

    _____   _____

7. Mount St. Helens, an active volcano, exploded in 1980. In what state is this volcano located? _____

8. In what state does the Mississippi River begin? _____

9. Into which large body of water does the Mississippi River flow? _____

10. In which direction does the Mississippi River flow? East to west, west to east, north to south, or south to north? _____

Use the reference sources you have learned about in this unit to answer the questions that follow. Choose the best reference source for each. Next to your answer, write the name of the book, CD-ROM, or the Internet address you used.

1. In which state was George Washington born?_____

   Reference Source_____

2. What is a synonym for *harmony* when used as a noun to mean a state of agreement?

   _____

   Reference Source_____

3. In what ocean would you find Easter Island?_____

   Reference Source_____

4. Who was the Greek god of the sea?_____

   Reference Source_____

5. What is the origin of the word *drama*?

   _____

   Reference Source_____

6. Which is the largest of the Hawaiian Islands?_____

   Reference Source_____

7. What is the capital of Zimbabwe?_____

   Reference Source_____

8. What is the main function of the human immune system?

   _____

   Reference Source_____

9. Which state has the most Electoral College votes?_____

   Reference Source_____

10. The Newbery Medal is awarded to the author of the best children's book. Which author won this award in 2007?_____

    What was the title of the book for which he or she won this award?

    _____

    Reference Source_____

11. What is the most common meaning of the word *honor*?

    _____

    Reference Source_____

12. In what year was gold discovered at Sutter's Mill in California?_____

    Reference Source_____

13. What country has the longest coastline?_____

    Reference Source_____

14. Which female singer earned the most money in 2006?_____

    Reference Source_____

15. Which is the tallest cactus in the world?_____

    Reference Source_____

Interpreting and Constructing Graphic Organizers and Charts

ACTIVITIES

Graphic organizers and charts are visual representations used to organize information. They help you to understand and remember information. In this unit, you will be learning about nine useful graphic organizers and charts.

A **topic-list graphic organizer** helps you organize information on a topic into its subtopics and details.

Read the following information about the features of the earth.

> Our planet earth has many distinguishing features. If you viewed the earth from above, you would immediately notice its mountains. Mountains may look solid and unchanging, but they are being built up and worn away by the weather all the time. The Andes is the longest mountain range. It stretches for more than 4,000 miles along the western side of South America. The Himalayas, located between India and the rest of Asia, has 20 of earth's highest mountains. One of these, Mt. Everest, is the highest mountain on earth.
>
> Earth has many islands. Some islands are the tops of undersea mountains. Others were once part of a large land mass but are now surrounded by water. Deserts are the driest places on earth. Most deserts are very hot. The largest desert is the Sahara Desert, which is in part of eleven countries of northern Africa. Whereas deserts are very dry, oceans are very wet. In fact, about 97 percent of all of the earth's water is in the oceans. There are five oceans. They all connect to make one large body of water.

Here are the steps to follow to construct a topic-list graphic organizer.

> 1. Draw a large oval in the middle of a page. Write the name of the topic in that oval.
> 2. Determine how many subtopics there are for the topic. Draw a slightly smaller oval for each subtopic arranged around the topic oval. Connect each subtopic oval to the topic oval with a line.
> 3. Write the name of each subtopic in one of the subtopic ovals.
> 4. Determine how many details there are for each subtopic.
> 5. Draw a slightly smaller oval for each detail either above or below the subtopic oval. Connect each detail oval with its subtopic oval with a line.
> 6. Write each detail in one of the detail ovals.

On the following page is the topic-list graphic organizer a student constructed based on the information provided about the features of the earth.

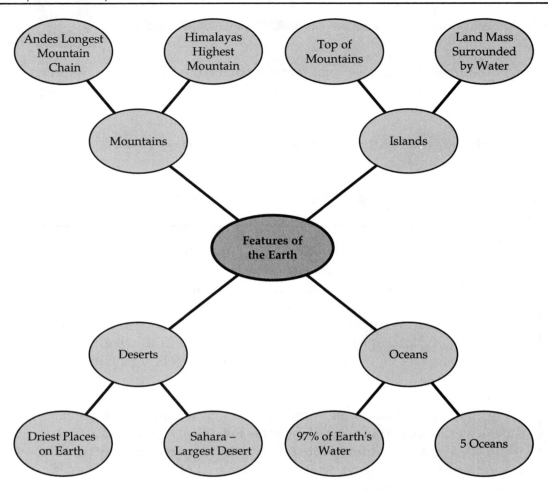

Read the following information about stars. Then complete the topic-list graphic organizer.

Stars

A star is a ball of gas that is so hot it burns and glows. If you look at the sky on a clear night, you will be able to see constellations of stars. The stars in each constellation are named after letters in the Greek alphabet. For thousands of years sailors used the stars to navigate. They were able to tell in which directions they were traveling.

Galaxies are giant groups of stars. Each galaxy consists of millions and even trillions of stars. Most galaxies are one of four shapes: spiral, irregular, oval, and elliptical. Our own galaxy is the Milky Way. It is made up of 100 billion stars. The Milky Way is in the shape of a spiral. Nebulae are seen as fuzzy patches of light as you look at the night sky. They are actually giant clouds of space dust and gas where new stars are born and old stars die. The Great Nebula of Orion can be seen with the naked eye.

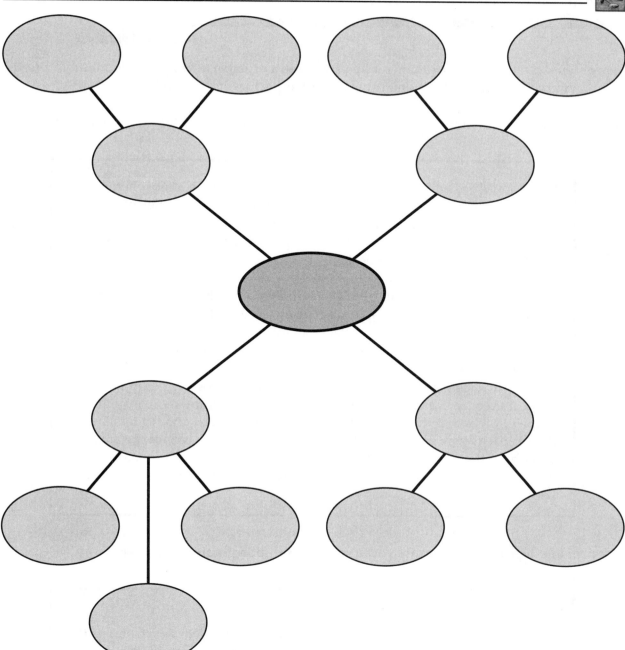

A **problem-solution graphic organizer** helps you see a problem, attempts at its solution, and the solution to the problem or the present status of attempts to solve the problem.

Read the following information about the problem of excessive greenhouse gas emissions.

Greenhouse gas emissions are emissions of gases into the atmosphere that affect the temperature and climate of the earth's surface. Scientists are concerned that increased emissions of these gases will have a negative impact on the earth's climate. The effect of excessive greenhouse gases is known as the "greenhouse effect."

Here are some of the things people are doing in their homes to reduce the greenhouse effect. Many people are replacing lightbulbs they use with ENERGY STAR bulbs (bulbs that are energy efficient). If every household changed just five bulbs, greenhouse gases would be greatly reduced. People are also buying ENERGY STAR products they use to heat and cool their homes. Replacing air filters regularly in heating and cooling equipment reduces greenhouse gas emissions. People are also adding more insulation to their homes to reduce the need to run air conditioners and heaters. In their gardens people are composting their yard waste to reduce the amount of garbage that is sent to landfills. Finally, people are taking numerous steps to use water more efficiently. Repairing all faucet leaks reduces water waste.

Here are the steps to follow to construct a problem-solution graphic organizer.

---

1. Write the problem in a box.
2. Write why it is a problem in a box below the problem box. Connect the two boxes with an arrow from the problem box to the why it is a problem box.
3. List all attempted solutions to the problem in a third box below the why it is a problem box. Connect the two boxes with an arrow from the why it is a problem box to the attempted solutions box.
4. Write the solution to the problem or the current status of attempted solutions in a fourth box below the attempted solutions box. Connect the two boxes with an arrow from the attempted solutions box to the solution or current status of the problem box.

On the next page is the problem-solution graphic organizer a student constructed about the problem of excessive greenhouse gas emissions.

Problem

> Excessive greenhouse gases

Why a Problem

> Can have a negative effect on the earth's climate.

Attempted Solutions

> Use ENERGY STAR lightbulbs and heating and cooling products
> > Replace air filters frequently
> > Add more insulation to homes
> > Reduce amount of garbage
> > Use water efficiently
> > Repair leaks

Solution or Status

> Until more steps are taken by more people, excessive greenhouse gas emissions will continue to be a problem.

Read the following information about the problem of the spread of bird flu. Then complete the problem-solution graphic organizer on the next page.

> The current deadly strain of bird flu (avian flu) was first seen in Hong Kong in 1997. Currently more than 150 million birds are affected. Humans can catch this flu by contact with live, infected birds. Because two out of three people who catch bird flu die, scientists and health professionals are very concerned the flu may spread around the world. As of now, there is no effective vaccine to protect people against bird flu.
>
> To stop a possible spread of bird flu, millions of infected birds have been destroyed. In some places birds are vaccinated. Farms on which infected birds are found are quarantined and disinfected. Wild birds are prevented from interacting with the domestic birds. Many countries ban the import of birds from countries where bird flu has been found.
>
> At this time bird flu has been contained. However, not enough is yet known about bird flu to enable scientists and health professionals to eliminate it.

Problem

Why a Problem

Attempted Solutions

Solution or Status

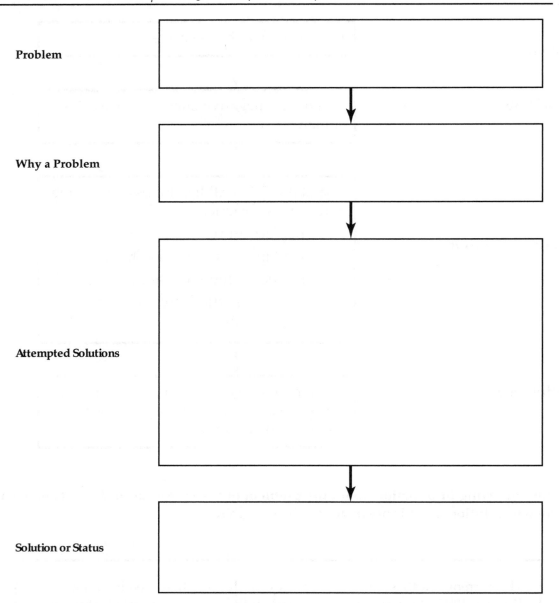

A **series of events graphic organizer** is helpful when you are working with historical information. This type of graphic organizer allows you to show the order in which events occurred along with details about each event.

Read the following passage about "The Early Americas."

The Early Americas

People first reached North America 15,000 to 20,000 years ago. They did this by crossing a land bridge that joined what today is called Asia with Alaska. The Olmec civilization developed in western Mexico between 1200 and 1400 BC. The Olmecs had a counting system and a calendar. They did not have a writing system. The Mayans built large pyramids in the centers of their cities between 600 BC and AD 250. These pyramids had small temples at the top. The Mayans were wonderful traders who travelled far and wide. From AD 100 to 700, the first great city developed in what is now Mexico. It was one of the largest cities in the world with a population of more than 250,000. The city was named Teotihuacán. Spanish conquerors destroyed this city and built a new city, which today is Mexico City.

Here are the steps to follow to construct a series of events graphic organizer.

---

1. Write the topic in a box in the middle of a sheet of paper.
2. Write the first of the events in a box. Label this box Event 1. Include any details about that event in the box. Connect this event box with a line to the topic box.
3. Construct similar boxes for the other events, labeling them Event 2, Event 3, and so on. Connect each of these boxes to the topic box.

Here is the series of events graphic organizer a student constructed about the Early Americas.

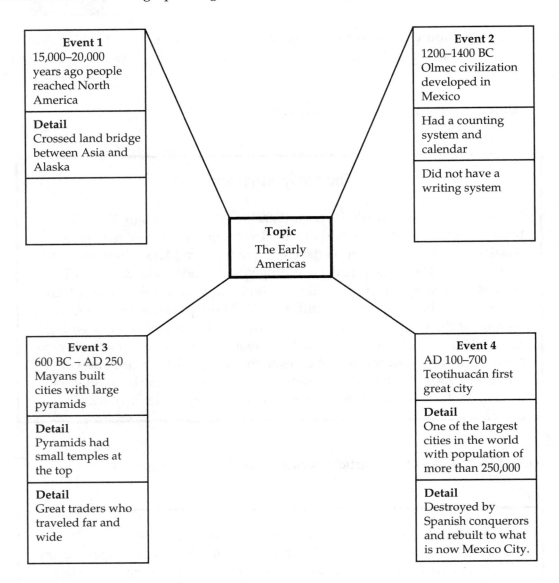

Event 1
15,000–20,000 years ago people reached North America

Detail
Crossed land bridge between Asia and Alaska

Event 2
1200–1400 BC Olmec civilization developed in Mexico

Had a counting system and calendar

Did not have a writing system

Topic
The Early Americas

Event 3
600 BC – AD 250 Mayans built cities with large pyramids

Detail
Pyramids had small temples at the top

Detail
Great traders who traveled far and wide

Event 4
AD 100–700 Teotihuacán first great city

Detail
One of the largest cities in the world with population of more than 250,000

Detail
Destroyed by Spanish conquerors and rebuilt to what is now Mexico City.

Read the following information about the Industrial Revolution. Then complete the series of events graphic organizer. You may find that you do not need to use all the boxes provided in the blank organizer on the next page.

The Industrial Revolution

The Industrial Revolution began about 1700 with the invention of machines for making cloth. The spinning jenny was one of the most important of these machines. It had to be turned by hand. In 1713, Abraham Darby discovered how to use coke instead of wood charcoal to produce iron. This made the production of huge amounts of iron much cheaper than before. In 1776, a machine for making cloth was invented that was driven by large water wheels. Several years later the world's first big factory was built using this machine. James Watt developed a steam engine to drive machines in the 1780s. As a result, steam replaced water as the main source of power in factories. When Henry Cort discovered how to remove impurities from iron in 1784, iron became the most important part of the Industrial Revolution.

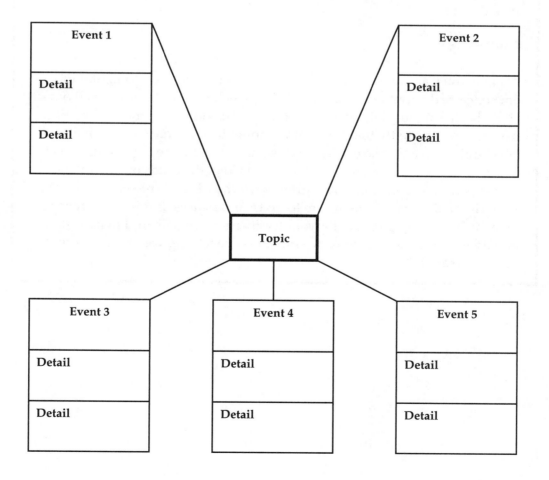

A **compare-contrast graphic organizer** is useful for showing how two things are both alike and different.

Read the following passage that compares the views of two candidates for political office.

CANDIDATE A

"Thank you for the opportunity to express my view on important issues. We are all concerned with terrorism. I believe we have to increase our war on terror. We have to stop terrorism, even if doing so interferes with our civil liberties. We can't stay involved in the affairs of every country in the Middle East. They will have to learn to take of their own business. I think that fair trade is a good thing. It opens up commerce and improves relations. We need to make sure that corporations do business around the world. Manufacturing our products in different parts of the world helps us because it keeps prices down. Finally, I'd like to say, we have to do everything we can to reduce global warming. We all must do our part to save the earth."

CANDIDATE B

"Thank you Candidate A and to all of you for coming here tonight. I too am concerned about terrorism. But I do not believe we should curtail our civil liberties in our fight against terrorism. The history of the Middle East has shown repeatedly that this region cannot take charge of its own affairs. We shouldn't try to take control, but we have to be there to provide direct assistance. Fair trade worries me. We haven't kept the needs of our American workers in mind. Our country grew with the idea of free enterprise. We shouldn't tell corporations where to do their business. If it is better for them to manufacture things out of the country, then so be it. Finally, I'm in complete agreement with candidate A; we must do everything we can to prevent global warming."

Here are the steps to follow to construct a compare-contrast graphic organizer.

1. Draw two boxes at the top of a sheet of paper.
2. In the left-hand box, write the name of one of the things you are comparing and contrasting.
3. In the right-hand box, write the name of the other thing you are comparing and contrasting.
4. Below the two boxes at the top, draw three evenly spaced vertical boxes that extend to the bottom of the page. Label the first and third boxes "Different" and the middle box "Same."
5. Draw a line from the top left-hand box to the left-hand "Different" box, and a second line to "Same" box.
6. Draw a line from the top right-hand box to the right-hand "Different" box, and a second line to "Same" box.
7. In the two boxes labeled "Different," write the differences between the two things you are comparing and contrasting.
8. In the two boxes labeled "Same," write how the two things you are comparing and contrasting are the same.

Here is the compare-contrast graphic organizer a student constructed about the views of the two candidates from the previous page.

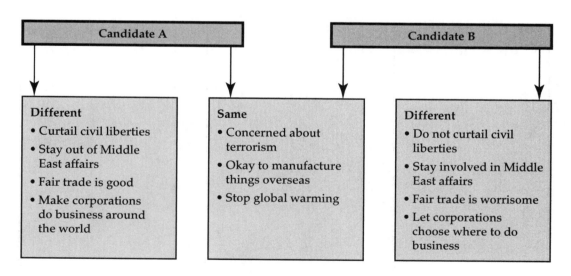

Read the following information about lions and tigers. Then complete the compare-contrast graphic organizer.

Lions are a member of the family Felidae. They belong to the species *Panthera leo*. Lions are found in both Africa and Asia. Lions live for about 10 to 14 years in the wild but can live longer in captivity. They typically inhabit savanna and grasslands. Lions are very social when compared to other big cats. They live in groups called prides. Prides consist of related females and offspring and a small number of adult males. Most of the hunting is done by the females in packs.

Tigers are also a member of the family Felidae. They belong to the species *Panthera tigris*. Tigers are found only in Asia. Tigers live 15 to 20 years in the wild and somewhat longer in captivity. They are quite comfortable living in savanna and grasslands. Tigers are not very social and prefer to live alone. Hunting is done equally by males and females.

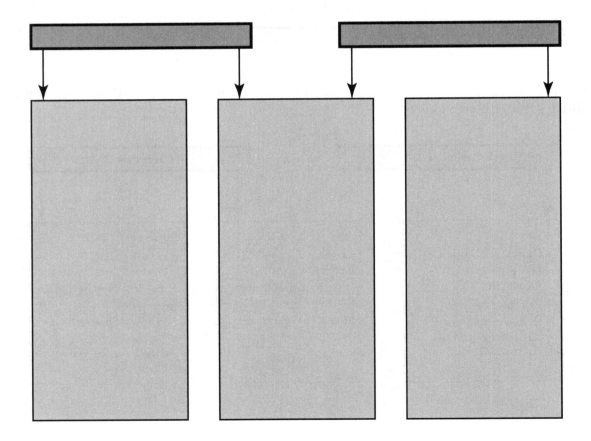

Question-Answer Graphic Organizer

A **question-answer graphic organizer** works well when you have questions about something.

Andrew's father mentioned that he had to go to the building supply store to buy some pressure-treated lumber. Andrew wanted to know why wood was pressure treated, how wood is pressure treated, and what safety measures should be taken when working with pressure-treated wood. He read the following article about pressure-treated lumber. Read the article yourself.

Wood is a great building material. However, many varieties of bacteria, fungi, and insects attack and eat wood. This is a big problem when lumber is stored on moist ground in lumberyards.

Pressure-treated lumber is wood that is immersed a liquid preservative and then placed in a pressure chamber. The pressure ensures that the chemical soaks deeply into the wood. The most common chemical used to treat lumber is a mixture of copper and arsenic called CCA. Wood that is not treated lasts only a year or two when in contact with moist ground. Wood treated with CCA can last decades.

Chemicals such as CCA used to treat wood can be dangerous to people. Warnings are posted to wear gloves when handling treated word, to avoid breathing sawdust produced when the wood is sawed, and to not burn the wood.

Here are the steps to follow to construct a question-answer graphic organizer.

---

1. Draw an oval at the top center of a sheet of paper. Write the heading "Topic" to the left of the oval. Write the topic in the oval.
2. Below the topic draw ovals going across for each of your questions. Write the heading "Questions" to the left of the first oval. Connect each oval by a line to the oval for the topic. Write a question in each oval.
3. Draw an oval below each oval for a question. Connect each oval by a line to the oval for its question. Write the heading "Answers" to the left of the first oval. Below each question, write the answer to the question in its oval.
4. Below each oval for an answer, draw an oval for each detail related to the answer. Connect each of these ovals to the oval for the answer the detail relates to. Write the heading "Details" to the left of the first oval. Write each detail in the appropriate oval.

After he read the article about pressure-treated lumber, Andrew constructed the question-answer graphic organizer shown on the next page.

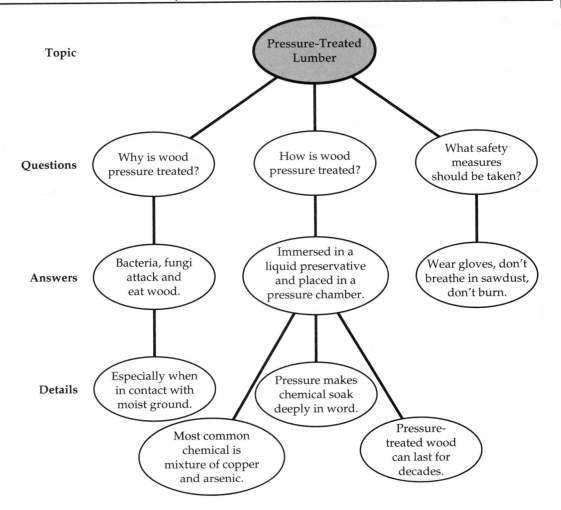

Suppose that when your class gets too noisy, your teacher has a habit of saying, "Keep those decibels down." You wanted to know what a decibel is, what the decibel level is for common sounds, and whether a sound that is too high in decibels can harm your hearing.

To answer these questions, you read the following encyclopedia article about decibels.

A decibel is the unit used to measure the intensity of a sound. It is abbreviated as dB. On the decibel scale, the smallest sound that can be heard is 0 dB. This is close to total silence. A sound that is ten times the intensity of 0 dB is rated as 10 dB. A sound 100 times in intensity is 20 dB, a sound 1000 times in intensity is 30 dB, and so on. Our normal conversation is 60 dB. When you mow the lawn the sound of the lawnmower is 90 dB. Have you ever attended a rock concert? The sound there can get as high as 120 dB. A firecracker set off on Independence Day comes in at 140 dB.

Any sound above 85 dB can cause hearing loss. The amount of hearing loss depends not just on the intensity of the sound, but also on how long you are exposed to the sound. If you are anywhere that you need to raise your voice for others to hear you, you will know that the sound around you is at least 85 dB.

Complete the question-answer graphic organizer for the encyclopedia article about decibels.

Topic

Questions

Answers

Details

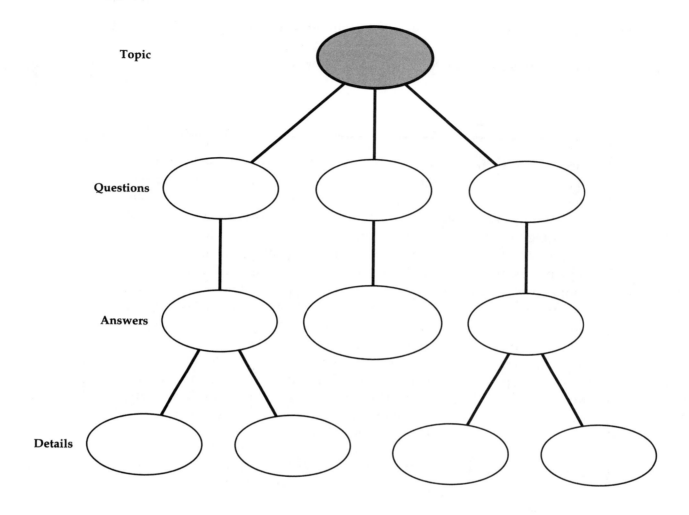

A cause-effect graphic organizer illustrates something that causes a number of effects.

Read the following passage about too many cars on the road.

> Cars are everywhere. You see them being driven on our roads, parked on our streets, and waiting to be purchased in new and used car lots. This may be good for the car manufacturers but not for us drivers. Why do I say this? Well, I've been late to work three times in the last month! Each time I left home on time but there was so much traffic that I could not move fast enough to arrive on time to my job. Quite clearly the tremendous number of cars on the road makes it very difficult to get from place to place. You can see the frustration on drivers' faces. Worse, sometimes we see road rage. A frustrated driver gets out of his car, starts screaming at another driver to move faster, and before you know it, a fight takes place. What finally gets them to stop fighting is they realize they can't breathe. Why can't they breathe? Well, the pollution from the gas exhaust produced by all the cars around them makes it difficult for them to draw a clean breath. They give up and get back in their cars because they are late to where they are going. So they try to speed up and begin to drive recklessly. You won't believe this, but their cars collide. Luckily they have only minor injuries. They look at each other, shrug their shoulders and say, "That's life today!" Unfortunately, many car accidents are of a serious nature. People are often badly hurt and sometimes killed.

Here are the steps to follows to construct a cause-effect graphic organizer.

1. At the top of a sheet of paper, write the headings "Cause," "Effects," and "Details" going across the page from left to right.
2. Draw a box under "Cause." Write the cause in the box.
3. Under "Effects," draw a box for each effect. Write each effect in its own box. Connect each of these boxes by a line to the box showing the cause.
4. For each effect, draw a box under "Details" for each detail related to the effect. Write each detail in its box. Connect each box by a line to the effect it relates to.

Here is the cause-effect graphic organizer a student constructed for the passage about too many cars on the road.

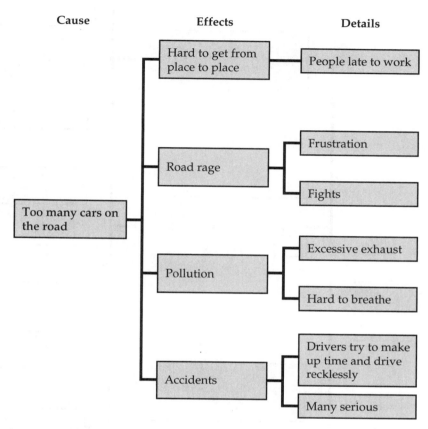

Read the following passage about not enough money for education. Then complete the cause-effect graphic organizer that follows on the next page.

Have you ever heard the expression, "Your tax dollars at work"? This expression is used by federal, state, and city governments to let us know they are putting the taxes we pay to good use. This is not true in the case of education. Not enough funding is provided to help schools give their students the best possible education.

There are several consequences of the underfunding of education. First, there are simply not enough schools because there is not enough money to build them. This results in overcrowded schools that have too many children in each room. Sometimes classes have to be held in the gym, auditorium, and even in the lunchroom. Some classrooms are portable structures located outside the main school building. These can be uncomfortably hot in the summer and cold in the winter. Another consequence of underfunding is that teachers are often not paid enough to keep them in their jobs. Many good teachers leave for higher-paying jobs, and it is difficult to recruit new teachers. Books and materials are often in short supply. Students often have to share a book, and teachers cannot purchase new books and materials, but have to make do with outdated versions. Student achievement is not as high as it should be. Many students act out their frustrations. Behavior then becomes a big problem that takes teachers' attention away from their teaching.

Cause	Effects	Details

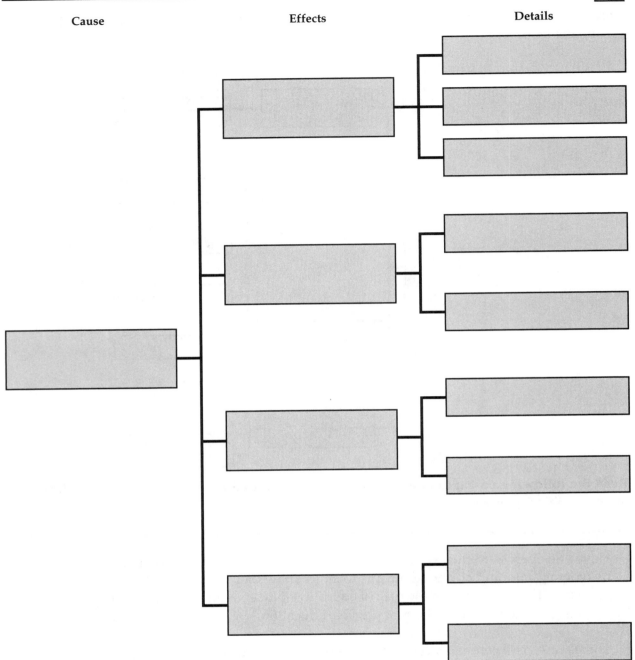

A **sequence chart** shows the steps to follow to accomplish something.

Read about the steps to follow when writing a research paper.

The first thing to do when writing a research paper is to select a topic. Your topic should not be too narrow or too broad. The next thing you must do is locate sources of information about your topic. These will be in both print and electronic form. As you locate each source of information, prepare bibliography cards to keep a record of the sources from which you obtain the information on note cards. Then write your first draft of the paper. Use a checklist to see the ways in which you must revise your draft. Write your final paper. Last, add a title page, table of contents, and bibliography.

Here are the steps to follow to construct a sequence chart.

1. Write the thing to be accomplished.
2. Write the first step.
3. Write each of the remaining steps up to the final step, each on its own line.
4. Write the final step.

Here is the sequence chart a student constructed to show the steps to follow when writing a research paper.

Thing to be Accomplished Write a research paper	
First	Select a topic. Should be not too narrow or broad.
Next	Locate sources of information in print and electronic form.
Next	Prepare bibliography cards.
Next	Prepare note cards.
Next	Write first draft.
Next	Use checklist to see what you must review.
Next	Write your final paper.
Last	Add title page, table of contents, and bibliography.

Read about the steps of a strategy for reading and taking notes from textbook chapters. Then complete the sequence chart.

> It is very important to have a strategy for reading and taking notes from textbook chapters. Here are the steps in an effective strategy for doing so. Begin by surveying your assigned chapter. Do this by reading the title, introduction, headings, and summary or conclusion. Then change the first heading into one or more questions and write the question(s). Use the words *who, what, where, when, why,* and *how* to form the questions. Next, read the information that follows the heading to find the answer(s) to the question(s) you wrote. Add one or more additional questions and their answer(s) as needed. Once you have done this, write the answer(s) to the question(s). Repeat the question-and-answer procedure for each heading in the chapter. Review your questions and answers as frequently as possible.

Thing to be Accomplished
First
Next
Next
Next
Next
Next
Next
Next
Last

A **five W's chart** is useful for organizing information found in a newspaper or magazine article.

Read the following newspaper article.

> **Polar bears vs. gas project in Alaska**
> **by Adam Williams**
> **Associated Press**
> **January 20, 2009**
>
> The polar bear can be found in just one place in America—Alaska. The federal government is considering listing polar bears as threatened under the Endangered Species Act. If the government does this, measures would be taken to protect the shrinking Arctic sea ice. Alaskans fear this would stop a proposed project to build a natural gas pipeline to tap Alaska's vast reserves. Sarah Palin, the governor of Alaska, issued a statement at a news conference in Anchorage yesterday opposing listing polar bears as threatened for this reason. Many state officials and newspaper reporters attended the conference. There is ongoing controversy as to whether the number of polar bears is decreasing.

Here is how to construct a five W's chart.

1. Draw a large box on a sheet of paper.
2. Draw horizontal lines to separate the box into five sections labeled in the following order: What happened? Who was there? Why did it happen? When did it happen? Where did it happen?
3. Write each answer in the appropriate section.

Here is the five W's chart a student constructed about the newspaper article.

What happened?
The governor of Alaska issued a statement opposing the federal government's plan to list the polar bear as threatened.

Who was there?
State officials and newspaper reporters.

Why did it happen?
The plan would interfere with Alaska's hope for a project to build a natural gas pipeline.

When did it happen?
January 20, 2009

Where did it happen?
Anchorage, AK

Read the following newspaper article and then complete the five W's chart that follows.

Timber toy town
By Lorraine Hawkins
Loveland Star
March 15, 2009

The Timber Dan Antique and Collectable Toy Show was held here in Loveland yesterday. The event brought together exhibitors from here in Colorado and nine other states. Many collectors from all over attended to buy and sell toys.

"Timber Dan" VanderLinden started the show in Loveland in the mid-1980s. He started the show because he became tired of traveling to toy shows all over the country. He started by collecting farm toys. Now living in Minnesota, he travels to Colorado to display and sell his toys.

The show has been a big success. Yesterday's event included 70 vendors. Profits from the show go the Lions Club.

What happened?	
Who was there?	
Why did it happen?	
When did it happen?	
Where did it happen?	

KWL Chart

A **KWL chart** is very useful when you are reading to learn about a topic.

The **K** stands for what you already know about the topic.
The **W** stands for what you want to learn about the topic.
The **L** stands for what you learn about the topic.

Here are the steps to follow to construct a KWL chart.

1. Draw a horizontal box across the top of a sheet of paper. Label this box "Topic." Write the topic you want to learn about in this box.
2. Draw three vertical boxes extending to the bottom of the page. Label the first box "K," the second box "W," and the third box "L."
3. Activate your prior knowledge about the topic. Think about what you already know and write this in the K column of the chart.
4. Write questions about what you want to know in the W column.
5. Read to find answers to the questions you wrote. Write the answers and any other useful information you learn in the L column.

Here is a KWL chart completed by a student about deserts.

Topic: Deserts

K	W	L
A desert has sand. It's hot in the desert. You find deserts where it's very dry.	Are there any plants living in the desert? What animals live in a desert? What is the largest desert?	Plants in the desert have long spreading roots to reach available moisture. These plants are designed to cut down on water loss from evaporation. There are animals. They usually hide from the heat during the day and come out at night. Camels live in the desert. They don't need much water. There is water in the desert that comes from underground streams. An area where this happens is called an oasis. The Sahara in North Africa is the largest desert in the world.

Choose a topic you want to learn about. Complete the KWL chart for this topic.

Topic:		
K	**W**	**L**

The names of the graphic organizers and charts you learned to construct are shown in the box.

Topic-List Graphic Organizer
Problem-Solution Graphic Organizer
Compare-Contrast Graphic Organizer
Cause-Effect Graphic Organizer
KWL Chart

Sequence Chart
Series of Events Graphic Organizer
Question-Answer Graphic Organizer
Five W'S Chart

For each of the following, write the name of the graphic organizer or chart that would be best to use. Use each graphic organizer or chart just once.

1. You have been studying the uses of electricity. You read to answer some questions you have about electricity.

   _____

2. You read an interesting article in your local newspaper about the hiring of a new school principal.

   _____

3. You are concerned about the problem of pollution. You read a book about how to reduce pollution.

   _____

4. You are studying the events that led to the American Civil War.

   _____

5. You took notes as your teacher described how to find the main idea in a paragraph.

   _____

6. You read about Republicans and Democrats and want to show how they are alike in some ways and different in other ways.

   _____

7. You want to read to learn more about sharks.

   _____

8. You have read a lot of information about how animals breed. You want to organize this information showing subtopics and details.

_____

9. You have read about how smoking can produce many health difficulties.

_____

Remembering Information

ACTIVITIES

7-1 Using the Rehearsal Strategy
7-2 Using the Visualization Strategy
7-3 Using the Grouping Strategy
7-4 Using the Rhyme Strategy
7-5 Using the Acronym Strategy
7-6 Using the First Letters Strategy
7-7 Using the Acronymic Sentence Strategy
7-8 Using the Pegwords Strategy
7-9 Using the Loci Strategy
7-10 Identifying the Remembering Strategy

Using the Rehearsal Strategy

In this unit, you will be learning about a number of strategies for remembering information. **Rehearsal** is a strategy you can use to learn information by rote. It is a good strategy to use to remember facts.

Here are the steps to follow when using the **rehearsal strategy**.

1. **Read** the information to be remembered.
2. **Write** the information.
3. **Say** the information.
4. **Repeat** the first three steps three or more times.

Fill in the blanks to show how to use the rehearsal strategy.

1. First,_____ the information.

2. Second,_____ the information.

3. Third,_____ the information.

4. Finally,_____ the steps at least_____ times.

Practice using the rehearsal strategy to remember the following information. Blank lines are provided for the writing you have to do in Step 2.

5. Zeus was the son of Cronus and Rhea.

   _____

   _____

   _____

6. The population of the world reached six billion in 1999.

   _____

   _____

   _____

7. Oslo is the capital of Norway.

   _____

   _____

   _____

8. A cat usually has 24 whiskers.

_____

_____

_____

9. Utah got its name from a Navajo word meaning "upper."

_____

_____

_____

10. E-mail was introduced in 1972.

_____

_____

_____

Visualization means to form a picture of something in your mind. It is a good strategy to use to remember information you read that you can easily picture in your mind.

Here are the steps to follow when using the **visualization strategy**.

> 1. **Read** the information.
> 2. **Picture** the information in your mind as you read.
> 3. **Plan** how to draw the information.
> 4. **Draw** the picture. Add labels if needed.
> 5. **Recall** the picture to remember the information.

Use the visualization strategy to remember the following description of an Arabian camel.

> An Arabian camel is a large animal that can be as tall as seven feet and weighs from 700 to 1,500 pounds. It lives in hot desert climates. The Arabian camel has a single large hump on its back and a beige or pale brown coat. The thick hair on its back offers it protection against the sun.
>
> The Arabian camel is an odd-looking animal to be sure. It has a curved neck, long slender legs, knobby knees, splayed feet, and a rounded chest. Long eyelashes and bushy eyebrows provide further protection from the blazing sun.

1. Cover the description and draw a picture of an Arabian camel as well as you can. Try to label its parts.

Without looking back at the written description of an Arabian camel, use the picture you drew to answer the following questions. Skip any questions you are unable to answer from the picture you drew.

2. In what type of environment would you be likely to find an Arabian camel?

   _____

3. What color is it?

   _____

4. What is the Arabian camel's chest like?

   _____

5. What feature of its eyebrows provides protection from the sun?

   _____

6. Where is its hair especially thick?

   _____

7. How many humps does it have?

   _____

8. What is its neck like?

   _____

9. What are its knees like?

   _____

10. Is the Arabian camel a tall or a short animal?

   _____

Grouping is a strategy for remembering information that can be grouped together. It is easier to remember information organized into groups in which all the items go together.

Here are the steps to follow when using the **grouping strategy**.

1. Look for ways the items of information to be remembered can be organized into groups in which all items go together.
2. Write an appropriate label for each group.
3. Under the label for each group, write the items that belong in that group in alphabetical order.
4. To remember the information, think of the label for the first group and the items that belong to that group. Repeat this for each of the other groups.

Here is an example of how to use the grouping strategy. Suppose your teacher presented some math words you should use in discussion at the next class session. You know what the words mean but will have to remember them to use them. Here are the words:

cube	gallon	sphere division	daylight	addition
noon	perimeter	plane millimeter	subtraction	ounce

Here are the words placed into groups with appropriate labels.

Geometry	**Measurement**	**Operations**	**Time**
cube	gallon	addition	daylight
perimeter	millimeter	division	noon
plane	ounce	subtraction	
sphere			

Complete each of the following.

1. Place each of these *descriptive words* in the appropriate group.

clatter	bitter	fuzzy	crash	sweet
stale	shaggy	delicious	bumpy	thud

Taste	**Touch**	**Sound**
_____	_____	_____
_____	_____	_____
_____	_____	_____
_____	_____	_____

2. Place each of these words relating to *sports* in the appropriate group.

touchdown   header   bunt   corner   kick   fault   tackle   volley
inning   fumble   throw-in   catcher   serve   pitcher

Football   **Baseball**   **Soccer**   **Tennis**

_____   _____   _____   _____

_____   _____   _____   _____

_____   _____   _____   _____

_____   _____   _____   _____

3. Place each of these names of *living things* into groups. Provide a label for each group.

Tuna   tabby   dalmatian   saluki   barracuda   oriole
terrier   minnow   roadrunner   rottweiler   salmon   swan
Persian   raven

_____   _____   _____   _____

_____   _____   _____   _____

_____   _____   _____   _____

_____   _____   _____   _____

_____   _____   _____   _____

4. Place these *food types* into groups. Provide a label for each group.

eggplant   kumquat   raspberry   rosemary   rice   pomegranate
tarragon   wheat   broccoli   cauliflower   barley   coriander
cucumber   oats   guava   garlic

_____   _____   _____   _____

_____   _____   _____   _____

_____   _____   _____   _____

_____   _____   _____   _____

Rhyme is a strategy for remembering information in which you write a poem that has corresponding sounds at the ends of the lines.

When Humpty Dumpty fell, what did he fall from? He fell from a wall, of course. How do we know that? We remember the rhyme:

> Humpty Dumpty sat on a wall.
> Humpty Dumpty had a great fall.

We know the spellings of the words *brief* and *ceiling* from the rhyme:

> i before e
> except after c

You do not have to be a poet to use the **rhyme strategy** to help you remember information. Just use your imagination and have some fun. Here is a rhyme to help remember the capital of Colorado.

> How can I possibly remember
> the capital of Colorado is Denver?

Use the rhyme strategy to remember the following information. A rhyming dictionary can help you do this.

1. The Pacific Ocean is the largest ocean.

   _____

   _____

   _____

   _____

2. The African elephant is the largest land mammal.

   _____

   _____

   _____

   _____

3. Jupiter is the planet in our solar system that has the most moons.

_____

_____

_____

_____

4. Crater Lake is the deepest lake in the United States.

_____

_____

_____

_____

5. China produces more fruit than any other country in the world.

_____

_____

_____

_____

6. The black mamba is the deadliest snake in the world.

_____

_____

_____

_____

7. More tourists visit France than any other country in the world.

_____

_____

_____

_____

8. The United States has more Web sites than any other country in the world.

_____

_____

_____

_____

9. Greenland is the largest island in the world.

_____

_____

_____

_____

10. The blue whale is the largest animal in the world.

_____

_____

_____

_____

An **acronym** is a word formed by using the first letter from a group of words. You can use the acronym strategy to remember a set of information by forming a word using the first letter of each piece of the information in the set. The acronym you form can be a real word or a nonsense word you are able to easily pronounce. Most often, the acronym you form will be a nonsense word.

The acronym strategy is a good strategy to use when information does not have to be remembered in a certain order. It is difficult to form an acronym for information that must be remembered in a certain order because the chances that the first letters will form a pronounceable word are small. Also, it is close to impossible to create an acronym if at least one of the pieces of information to be remembered does not begin with a vowel.

Here is how to use the **acronym strategy**.

---

1. **Write** each piece of information you need to remember.
2. **Underline** the first letter of each piece of information. If there is more than one word in a piece of information, underline the first letter of the first word only.
3. **Arrange** the underlined letters to form a real word or a nonsense word you can easily pronounce.
4. **Recall** the acronym you formed and the piece of information represented by each letter in the acronym whenever you need to remember the information.

HOMES is an example of an acronym you can use to remember the names of the five Great Lakes in any order: Erie, Superior, Michigan, Ontario, and Huron. In HOMES, **H** is the first letter of **Huron**, **O** the first letter of **Ontario**, and so on.

You can use the acronym "thop" to remember the following types of polygons in any order: hexagon, tetragon, pentagon, and octagon. "Thop" is not a real word, but you can easily pronounce it. Notice that you cannot form a real word using the first letter of each type of polygon to be remembered.

Sometimes, more than one of the pieces of information you must remember begins with the same first letter. The acronym "rider" can be used to remember the following five body systems in any order: digestive, respiratory, endocrine, reproductive, and immune. You can use the first "r" in this acronym to remember either "respiratory" or "reproductive" and the second "r" to remember the other.

Form an acronym for each of the following sets of information. The pieces of information in each set can be remembered in any order. The acronym you form can be a real word or a nonsense word you can easily pronounce.

1. *Types of maps:* weather, economic, political, road

   _____

2. *Time zones:* eastern, central, mountain, pacific

   _____

3. *Measures of length:* inch, foot, furlong, mile, yard

   _____

4. *Words ending with "onym":* homonym, acronym, synonym, pseudonym, eponym

   _____

5. *Cabinet departments:* defense, commerce, education, agriculture, treasury

   _____

6. *Countries in South America:* Bolivia, Chile, Argentina, Ecuador, Columbia

   _____

7. *World capitals:* Belgrade, Ottawa, Kampala, Managua, Amman

   _____

8. *State flowers:* rose, lilac, camellia, iris, apple blossom

   _____

As you learned on Activity **7-5**, it is difficult to form an *acronym* when information must be remembered in a certain order or the letters to be used do not contain at least one vowel. In both cases, the **first letters strategy** can be used instead.

Here is how to use the first letters strategy.

> 1. **Write** the pieces of information in the order in which you must remember them.
> 2. **Underline** the first letter of each item of information. If there is more than one word in an item of information, underline the first letter of only the first word in that piece of information.
> 3. **Write** the underlined letters in their order to form an abbreviation.

For example, imagine that when studying United States geography, you are required to remember the four largest states in area in order from largest to smallest.

Here are the names of the four largest states and each state's total area in square miles (land + water).

State	Area
California	163,696
Montana	145,552
Alaska	663,267
Texas	268,581

The order in which you would have to remember these states is: <u>A</u>laska, <u>T</u>exas, <u>C</u>alifornia, and <u>M</u>ontana.

The first letters in their order you would write to remember this information are **ATCM**

Later, to remember these four states in order of their area from highest to lowest, think of the first letters **ATCM**. The **A** will help you recall that Alaska has the largest area; the **T** that Texas is next, and so on.

Write the first letters in appropriate order for each of the following.

1. Here are the four most commonly spoken languages in the world. The number of speakers is shown rounded to the nearest million. Write the first letter of each language to help you remember these four languages *in order beginning with the highest number of speakers*.

English	309 million
Hindi	181 million
Mandarin	873 million
Spanish	322 million

   First letters _____

2. Here are the number of calories in average portions of five types of meat. Write the first letter of each type of meat to help you remember these types of meat *in order of lowest to highest number of calories.*

beef	360
chicken	220
lamb	300
pork	320
liver	200

First letters _____

3. Here are five inventions and the year in which each was invented. Write the first letter of each invention to remember these inventions *in order starting with the earliest invention.*

helicopter	1938
sewing machine	1845
dynamite	1866
parachute	1785
escalator	1891

First letters _____

4. Here are five states and the year in which each became part of the United States. Write the first letter of each state to remember these states *in the order they joined the United States from most recent to the earliest.*

Virginia	1788
Hawaii	1959
Delaware	1787
Kentucky	1792
Indiana	1816

First letters _____

5. Here are six former presidents of the United States and the year in which each became president. Write the first letter of the name of each president to remember *the order in which they became president from earliest to most recent.*

Harrison	1841
Lincoln	1861
Hayes	1877
Jefferson	1801
Carter	1977
Kennedy	1961

First letters _____

6. Here are the average incomes per person for six countries. Write the first letter of each country to remember these countries *in order of average income per person from highest to lowest.*

Turkey	$7,900
Ecuador	$3,900
United States	$42,000
Denmark	$33,400
Argentina	$13,700
Mexico	$10,100

First letters _____

The **acronymic sentence strategy** is equally useful for remembering information in any order or in a certain order. It is similar to the *acronym strategy* you learned to use in Activity **7-5**. The difference is that the first letter of each piece of information to be remembered is used to form a sentence rather than a word.

Here is how to use the acronymic sentence strategy.

---

1. **Write** each piece of information you need to remember.
2. **Underline** the first letter of each piece of information. If there is more than one word in a piece of information, underline the first letter of the first word only.
3. **Write** a sentence using words that begin with the underlined letters. If you must remember the information in a certain order, the order of the words in the sentence you create must be consistent in the order in which you must remember the pieces of information.

Try to create a sentence that will be easy for you to remember. A good idea is to create a sentence that has special meaning to you or that is funny or unusual.

Here is an example of an acronymic sentence created to remember the following "fun" holidays *in any order*: Groundhog Day, Mother's Day, Father's Day, Halloween, and Valentine's Day.

Victoria gave me four hamburgers.

Later, to remember these five holidays, you would recall this sentence. The "V" in Victoria would help you remember "Valentine's Day," the "g" in gave would help you remember "Groundhog Day," and so on.

Now, here is an example of an acronymic sentence created to remember the five oceans of the world *as shown in order* of their size from largest to smallest: Pacific, Atlantic, Indian, Southern, and Arctic.

Put all instruments safely away.

It was more difficult to create this acronymic sentence than to create an acronym for the first example because the order of the words in this sentence had to be in a certain order.

Write an acronymic sentence to help you remember each of the following.

1. The five senses in any order: hearing, sight, touch, smell, and taste.

_____

_____

2. The birth countries of immigrants to the United States as shown in order from the highest to the fifth highest: Mexico, India, China, Philippines, and Cuba.

_____

_____

3. Five ancient Greek gods in any order: Zeus, Apollo, Aphrodite, Hermes, and Poseidon.

_____

_____

4. The birthstones for the first five months of the year as shown in order from January to May: garnet, amethyst, aquamarine, diamond, and emerald.

_____

_____

5. Six types of literature in any order: autobiography, fantasy, legend, fiction, nonfiction, and myth.

_____

_____

6. The sixth largest planets in our solar system as shown in order from largest to smallest: Jupiter, Saturn, Uranus, Neptune, Earth, and Venus.

_____

_____

The **pegwords strategy** is useful for remembering numbered information such as four causes of the American Civil War. *Pegwords* are words that rhyme with number words. Each pegword is substituted for a number word and is associated with the information to be remembered.

Here are suggested pegwords for the number words one through ten. You can substitute your own pegwords as long as each rhymes with its corresponding number word.

Number Word	*Pegword*
one	run
two	shoe
three	tree
four	door
five	hive
six	sticks
seven	heaven
eight	gate
nine	sign
ten	pen

You can use any word as a pegword as long as it rhymes with a number word. You can substitute your own pegwords. Nouns or verbs are best because they can be easily used to form many associations with the information you want to remember.

Here is how to use the pegwords strategy.

1. **Think** of the first piece of information you must remember.
2. **Think** of the pegword for the number *one*. The pegword for *one* is *run*.
3. **Form** an association in your mind between the pegword *run* and the first piece of information you must remember. Create a picture in your mind of this association.
4. **Repeat** steps 1 to 3 for each additional piece of information you must remember. Substitute the pegword *shoe* for the second piece of information, *tree* for the third piece, and so on.

Here is an example of how the pegwords strategy can be used to remember four long-term effects of the Industrial Revolution.

Here are the four effects:

1. Many people moved from the countryside to cities to find work.

2. People now enjoy a higher standard of living.

3. Pollution.

4. Depletion of natural resources such as coal, oil, and minerals.

The pegword for *one* is *run*. To remember that people moved from the countryside to the city to find work, associate this effect with *run*. For example, create a picture in your mind in which people are running from a farm to a city that has big factories with smoke coming from their smokestacks.

Here are pictures you could create in your mind for the next three effects.

(two/shoe) People enjoy a higher standard of living. Create a picture in your mind of a man or a woman walking toward a store. The sign on the store says "Very Expensive Shoes."

(three/tree) Pollution. Create a picture in your mind of a park in which leaves are falling from tree branches. There is a sign at the park entrance that reads "Caution: High Smog Alert."

(four/door) Depletion of natural resources. Create a picture in your mind of an apartment building with a sign on the entrance door that reads "No heat today. Out of oil."

1. Describe the pictures you would create in your mind when using the pegwords strategy to remember the following five characteristics of cats.

One: Cats are excellent hunters.

_____

_____

_____

Two: Cats are very curious or inquisitive.

_____

_____

_____

Three: Cats spend at least an hour a day grooming their fur by licking it with their tongues.

_____

_____

_____

Four: Cats sleep almost twice as many hours a day as do other animals.

_____

_____

_____

Five: Cats have an excellent sense of smell.

_____

_____

_____

2. Describe the pictures you would create in your mind when using the pegwords strategy to remember the following five objects that are manufactured from recycled materials.

One: bicycles from recycled steel

_____

_____

_____

Two: newspapers from recycled paper

_____

_____

_____

Three: speed bumps from recycled rubber

_____

_____

_____

Four: milk containers from plastic

_____

_____

_____

Five: jars from recycled glass

_____

_____

_____

Loci is the plural form of locus, which means place. You can easily remember features of places you are very familiar with, such as your house or apartment. The **loci strategy** is based on your familiarity with a place. It is a good strategy to use if you are good at visualizing or picturing things.

Here is how to use the loci strategy.

---

1. **Think** of a place you know very well.
2. **Visualize** the features of that place.
3. **Visualize** each piece of information you want to remember as associated with one of the features. Make the association as unusual as possible.
4. **Visualize** each feature of the place and the piece of information you associated with it to recall the pieces of information.

For example, suppose you wanted to remember six words that will be on your next spelling test. You decide to use the kitchen of your house as the familiar place.

Here are the six spelling words to remember: nature, invasion, pigeon, lemon, puddle, and somersault.

Here is what you might visualize for each word:

> *nature*–visualize a tree growing out of the coffeepot on the counter.
> *invasion*–visualize ants swarming all over a slice of bread on the table.
> *pigeon*–visualize a pigeon landing on the windowsill.
> *lemon*–visualize lemons floating in a pitcher of water inside the refrigerator.
> *puddle*–visualize the sink overflowing and producing a puddle of water on the floor.
> *somersault*–visualize a little child somersaulting over a kitchen chair.

To recall the words, visualize the features of the kitchen. As you do, the word you associated with that feature will come to mind.

The loci strategy can easily be adapted to remember pieces of information in a certain *order*. To do this, use a familiar route from one place to another rather than a place. Visualize features along the route in the order you would come to them. Associate the first piece of information to be remembered with the first feature along the route, the second piece of information with the second feature along the route, and so on.

For example, suppose you had to remember the five best-selling children's books through 2000 in order starting with the highest selling as shown.

> *The Poky Little Puppy*
> *The Tale of Peter Rabbit*
> *Tootle*
> *Green Eggs and Ham*
> *Harry Potter and the Goblet of Fire*

You decide to remember these books in order using the route you take from home to school. The first five features that come to mind along this route are a large oak tree, a supermarket, a bus stop, a restaurant, and a fire station.

Here is what you might visualize for each book:

> To remember *The Poky Little Puppy*, you could visualize a puppy trying to climb a tree.
>
> To remember *The Tale of Peter Rabbit*, you could visualize a rabbit eating carrots from a vegetable bin inside a supermarket.
>
> To remember *Tootle*, you could visualize a train pulling into a bus stop.
>
> To remember *Green Eggs and Ham*, you could visualize yourself seated inside a restaurant about to eat a plate of green eggs and ham.
>
> To remember *Harry Potter and the Goblet of Fire*, you could visualize firemen rushing out of a fire station to put out a fire that is raging in a very large goblet.

1. Use the loci strategy to remember these football teams in any order: Chicago Bears, Indianapolis Colts, New York Giants, Philadelphia Eagles, Miami Dolphins, and Denver Broncos.

   Write the name of the place you are using: _____

   Identify the feature of the place and describe the picture you formed in your mind to remember each team:

   Chicago Bears

   Feature: _____

   Picture: _____

   _____

   _____

Indianapolis Colts

Feature: _____

Picture: _____

_____

_____

New York Giants

Feature: _____

Picture: _____

_____

_____

Eagles

Feature: _____

Picture: _____

_____

_____

Miami Dolphins

Feature: _____

Picture: _____

_____

_____

Denver Broncos

Feature: _____

Picture: _____

_____

_____

2. Use the loci strategy to remember these six baseball teams in order of most wins in 2007 to least wins: Cleveland Indians (96 wins), Toronto Blue Jays (83 wins), Minnesota Twins (79 wins), Florida Marlins (71 wins), Boston Red Sox (96 wins), and Pittsburgh Pirates (68 wins).

What route are you using? From _____ To _____

Identify the feature of the route and describe the picture you formed in your mind to remember each team.

Name of team with most wins _____

Feature: _____

Picture _____

_____

_____

Name of team with next most wins _____

Feature: _____

Picture _____

_____

_____

Name of team with next most wins _____

Feature: _____

Picture _____

_____

_____

Name of team with next most wins _____

Feature: _____

Feature: _____

Picture _____

_____

_____

Name of team with next most wins _____

Feature: _____

Picture _____

_____

_____

Name of team with least wins _____

Feature: _____

Picture _____

_____

_____

Identifying the Remembering Strategy

You have learned nine strategies for remembering information: rehearsal, visualization, grouping, rhyme, acronym, first letters, acronymic sentences, pegwords, and loci. Let's see how well you have learned these strategies.

Complete each of the following by writing the name of the strategy that is being used. Each of the strategies is used once.

1. William must remember the following features of the flag of the United States: (1) its colors are red, white, and blue; (2) it has 50 stars; (3) it has 13 stripes; and (4) it is flown at half-mast as a sign of national mourning. He associates these features with the number words one through four.

   William is using the _____ strategy.

2. Felipe must remember the names of these types of scientists in any order: astronomer, meteorologist, geologist, and epidemiologist. He uses the first letter of the name of each scientist to form the word "game."

   Felipe is using the _____ strategy.

3. Margaret must remember that Tokyo is the capital of Japan. She writes this fact and recites it several times.

   Margaret is using the _____ strategy.

4. Antoine must remember what the White House looks like. He forms a picture of the White House in his mind as he reads a description of it. He then draws a picture of the White House

   Antoine is using the _____ strategy.

5. Lois must remember the following characteristics of Australia: it is an island, cricket is a very popular sport, meat is a favorite food, and most children wear uniforms to school. She associates each of these characteristics with a feature of her school.

   Lois is using the _____ strategy.

6. Alex must remember that George Washington was once a soldier. To remember this, he writes a poem that has corresponding sounds at the end of each line.

   Alex is using the _____ strategy.

7. Melissa must remember the four fastest fish in the order shown: sailfish, marlin, bluefin tuna, and yellowfin tuna. She writes the following sentence. Some men buy yo-yos.

   Melissa is using the _____ strategy.

8. Cassandra must remember the four most common last names in the United States population. She must remember them in order from most common to fourth most common (Smith, Johnson, Williams, Jones). Cassandra writes the first letter of each name in order.

   Cassandra is using the _____ strategy.

9. Ashley must remember to buy the following items for a picnic: mustard, ham, bologna, juice, ketchup, bread, salami, cake, hot sauce, water, and rolls. She groups these items under: baked goods, meats, and drinks.

   Ashley is using the _____ strategy.

Taking Tests

ACTIVITIES

An objective test is a test that contains items requiring very short responses. Objective tests are also known as short-answer tests. In this unit you will be learning about four types of objective tests: multiple-choice, true/false, matching, and completion.

DETER is a strategy that will help you do your best on each of these types of tests. Each letter in DETER stands for a step in the strategy. Read to learn the five steps in DETER.

D	Read the test **Directions** carefully. Ask your teacher to explain any directions or words you do not understand.
E	**Examine** the entire test to see how much there is to do.
T	Decide how much **Time** to spend answering each question.
E	Answer the questions you find **Easiest** first.
R	**Review** your answers to be sure they are your best answers and that you answered all required questions.

For each letter in the DETER strategy, write a statement that tells what you should do for that step of the strategy. Underline the most important word in each statement you write.

D _____

_____

E _____

_____

T _____

_____

E _____

_____

R _____

_____

A **multiple-choice test** requires you to choose an answer from a set of possible answers. There are two types of items you will find on multiple-choice tests. The first type of item presents an incomplete statement followed by several answer choices. You are to circle the letter of the answer choice that correctly completes the statement. There are usually four answer choices, but there can be more.

Look at the following example. In this example you should circle the letter "c" because there are 50 states in the United States.

There are _____ states in the United States.

   a. 40
   b. 48
   c. 50
   d. 52

The second type of multiple-choice item presents a question followed by several answer choices. You are to circle the letter of the answer choice that correctly answers the question.

Look at the following example. In this example, you should circle "b."

How many states are in the United States?

   a. 40
   b. 50
   c. 48
   d. 52

Sometimes an answer choice is "None of the above." Look at the following example. In this example, "None of the above" is the correct answer choice because none of the countries shown as an answer choice are located in Europe.

Countries located in Europe include_____.

   a. China
   b. Canada
   c. Bolivia
   d. None of the above

Sometimes an answer choice is "All of the above." Look at the following example. In this example, "All of the above" is the correct answer choice because France, Germany, and Italy are all located in Europe.

> Which of the following countries is located in Europe?
>
> a. France
> b. Germany
> c. Italy
> d. All of the above

Use the information in the box that follows to write two multiple-choice test items. Your first item should be an *incomplete statement* followed by four answer choices. Your second item should be a *question* followed by four answer choices.

> *Year:* 1775
>
> *Event:* The American Revolution began.

1. _____

   a. _____

   b. _____

   c. _____

   d. _____

2. _____

   a. _____

   b. _____

   c. _____

   d. _____

Here are guidelines that will help you do well when taking a multiple-choice test. Read these guidelines and use them when you take the practice multiple-choice test that follows.

- *Circle or underline important words in the item.* Doing this will help you make sure you have read the statement or question carefully.
- *Read all the answer choices before selecting one.* It is just as likely for the last answer choice to be correct as it is for the first answer choice to be correct.
- *Cross out any answer choices you are certain are incorrect.* This will help you to narrow down the correct answer choice.
- *Look for answer choices that contain absolute terms such as* **all, always,** *and* **never.** An answer choice that contains an absolute term is usually *not* the correct answer choice.
- *Look for two answer choices that are the opposite of each other.* One of these answer choices is usually correct.
- *When answering an item, look for hints about the correct answer in other items on the test.* Sometimes the correct answer choice for an item is contained in the statement or question for a different item.
- *Look for answer choices that contain language used by your teacher or found in your textbook.* An answer choice that contains such language is usually correct.
- *Select "All of the above" as an answer choice only if you are certain that all other answer choices are correct.* If even just one of the other answer choices is incorrect, "All of the above" is not the correct answer choice.
- *Select "None of the above" as an answer choice only if you are certain that all other answer choices are incorrect.* If even just one of the other answer choices is correct, "None of the above" is not the correct answer choice.
- *Do not change your answer unless you are sure that a different answer choice is better.* Often your first choice is the correct answer choice.
- *Answer all items unless there is a penalty for incorrect answers.* If there is no penalty, use the guidelines above to make your best guess.

Take the following multiple-choice test. This test is on the guidelines for taking multiple-choice tests you just learned.

Directions Circle the letter in front of the answer choice you believe is correct. There is no penalty for incorrect answers.

1. Change your answer only when you are sure a different answer choice is _____.

   a. longer

   b. better

   c. incorrect

   d. shorter

2. Choose "All of the above" as the answer choice when _____.

    a. some of the other answer choices are correct

    b. most of the other answer choices are incorrect

    c. all of the other answer choices are correct

    d. none of the other answer choices are correct

3. You should _____ an answer choice when you decide it is not correct.

    a. choose

    b. reread

    c. rewrite

    d. cross out

4. When should you answer all items?

    a. When you are running out of time.

    b. When there is no penalty for incorrect answers.

    c. When there is a penalty for incorrect answers.

    d. When you don't understand some of the items.

5. When two answer choices are _____, one of them is usually correct.

    a. difficult

    b. easy

    c. opposites

    d. short

6. When should you select an answer choice?

    a. After you have read all of the answer choices.

    b. As soon as you come to what you think is the correct answer choice.

    c. After you have reread the statement or question.

    d. After you have crossed out one answer choice.

7. Sometimes you can find a hint about the correct answer to an item by_____.

   a. looking at your answers to other items on the test

   b. counting the number of words in an item

   c. counting the number of words in each answer choice

   d. looking at the statements or questions in other items on the test

8. Circle or underline _____ words in the statement or question.

   a. technical

   b. unknown

   c. important

   d. long

9. Choose "None of the above" as the answer choice when _____.

   a. some of the other answer choices are correct

   b. most of the other answer choices are incorrect

   c. all of the other answer choices are correct

   d. none of the other answer choices are correct

10. An answer choice is likely to be correct if it contains _____.

   a. information from a newspaper

   b. words found in popular magazines

   c. language used in your textbook

   d. words you do not understand

11. Which type of term in an answer choice usually means that the answer choice is incorrect?

   a. A scientific term

   b. A mathematical term

   c. A long term

   d. An absolute term

Score your test as your teacher goes over the answers. Your score for the test is your number correct. Enter your score in the box below to see how well you did.

My Score _____
10–11 = Excellent
8–9 = Good
0–7 = Review the guidelines.

True/false tests require you to read statements and decide whether each statement is *true* or *false*. True/false test items seem easy because you have a 50/50 chance of guessing the correct answer. However, true/false test items can be very difficult because they test for specific factual information.

Here are guidelines that will help you do well when taking a true/false test. Read these guidelines, and use them when you take the practice true/false test that follows.

- ***Choose* true *for a test item unless you can prove that the statement is* false.** For a statement to be *true*, everything in the statement must be *true*.
  For example, the following statement is *true* because all three planets are part of our solar system.
  Saturn, Mercury, and Venus are planets in our solar system.
  The following statement is *false* because Oceania is not a planet in our solar system.
  Saturn, Mercury, and Oceania are planets in our solar system.

- ***Carefully reread statements that contain a negative word such as* not *or that contain a word that begins with a negative prefix such as "un-," as in* unfriendly.** Negative words or prefixes completely change the meaning of a statement.
  For example, the following two statements look very similar, yet the first statement is *true* and the second is *false* because of the word "not."
  The rattlesnake is a poisonous snake.
  The rattlesnake is not a poisonous snake.
  In the following statements, the first statement is *true*, whereas the second statement is *false* because of the prefix "dis-" that begins the word "dishonest."
  Our society should reward a politician who is honest.
  Our society should reward a politician who is dishonest.

- ***If a statement has two negatives, cross out both negatives.*** Two negatives make a positive, but in a confusing way. Crossing out the two negatives will make it easier for you to understand the meaning of the statement. Read the two statements that follow. Both are *true*. The second statement is easier to understand because the two negatives have been crossed out.
  You will not get good grades if you do not study.
  You will ~~not~~ get good grades if you do ~~not~~ study.

- ***Absolute statements are usually* false. *Qualified statements are usually* true.** Absolute statements include words such as the following: *all, none, always,* and *every*. Qualified statements include words such as *some, many, usually,* and *most*.
  Read the following two statements. The absolute word *all* in the first statement makes this statement *false*. Replacing *all* with the qualified word *some* in the second statement makes the statement *true*.
  All the planets in our solar system have one or more moons.
  Some of the planets in our solar system have one or more moons.

- ***If you are uncertain whether a statement is* true *or* false, *take your best guess unless there is a penalty for incorrect answers.*** In most true/false tests there are usually more *true* statements than *false* statements. If you are completely undecided between *true* and *false*, choose *true* as the answer.

Take the following true/false test. This test is on the guidelines for taking true/false tests that you just learned.

Directions Circle TRUE or FALSE in front of each statement. There is a one-point deduction for each incorrect answer.

TRUE   FALSE   **1.** A negative word can completely change the meaning of statement.

TRUE   FALSE   **2.** Absolute statements are usually false.

TRUE   FALSE   **3.** Most parts of a statement must be true for a statement to be true.

TRUE   FALSE   **4.** If you are not certain a statement is false, consider it true.

TRUE   FALSE   **5.** Qualified statements are usually true.

TRUE   FALSE   **6.** If a statement has two negatives, you should cross out one of the negatives.

TRUE   FALSE   **7.** If there is penalty for incorrect answers, you should make your best guess.

TRUE   FALSE   **8.** You will most likely not do well on a true/false test if you cannot understand the statements.

Score your test as your teacher goes over the answers. Subtract your number incorrect from your number correct to get your score for the test. Enter your score in the box below to see how well you did.

My Score _____
7–8 = Excellent
5–6 = Good
0–4 = Review the guidelines.

Taking Matching Tests

A **matching test** requires you to match words or terms in one column with words or terms in a second column. Usually you have to match the words or terms in the right-hand column with those in the left-hand column. In the following matching test, the answers have been provided.

Directions On the line to the left of each name of a science, write the letter found next to what is studied in that science.

Science	What Is Studied
1. <u>b</u> Zoology	**a.** plants
2. <u>c</u> Mineralogy	**b.** animals
3. <u>d</u> Genetics	**c.** minerals
4. <u>a</u> Botany	**d.** heredity

Sometimes there may be more words or terms in the right-hand column than in the left-hand column. This means that not every word or term in the right-hand column can be used as a match. Here is an example of this type of matching test with the answers provided.

Directions On the line to the left of the name of each sports team, write the letter found next to the sport the team plays. There are two more sports played than sports teams.

Sport Team	Sport Played
1. <u>e</u> Montreal Canadiens	**a.** basketball
2. <u>c</u> New York Yankees	**b.** football
3. <u>a</u> Boston Celtics	**c.** baseball
4. <u>b</u> Green Bay Packers	**d.** soccer
	e. hockey
	f. tennis

Here are guidelines that will help you do well when taking a matching test. Read these guidelines and use them when you take the practice matching test that follows.

- *Read all the words or terms in both columns before making any matches.* If you make the first match that looks possible, you may not choose the correct match.
- *Start by making matches for the information about which you are certain.* This will reduce the number of choices for the words or terms about which you are not certain.
- *Cross out words or terms in both columns as you make matches.* This reduces the amount of information you will have to consider for the remaining matches.
- *Make your best guess at any remaining matches only when there is no penalty for incorrect matches.* Penalties can lower your score for the test.
- *Carefully review your matches when you have completed the test.* Reviewing the matches you made is important because one incorrect match may result in another match being incorrect.

Take the following matching test. This test is on the guidelines you just learned.

Directions   On the line to the left of each beginning of a guideline for taking matching tests, write the letter found next to the ending that completes the guideline. There is no penalty for incorrect answers.

Beginning

1. _____ Make your best guess at any remaining matches

2. _____ Carefully review your matches

3. _____ Read all the words or terms in both columns

4. _____ Cross out items in both columns

5. _____ Start by making matches

Ending

a. for the information about which you are certain.

b. when you have completed the test.

c. even if you are uncertain.

d. only when there is no penalty for incorrect matches.

e. before making any matches.

f. as you make matches.

Score your test as your teacher goes over the answers. Your score is your number correct. Enter your score in the box to see how well you did.

> My score_____
> 5 = Excellent
> 4 = Good
> 0–3 = Review the guidelines.

A **completion test** consists of items in which part of the statement is missing. The missing part of the statement is indicated by a blank line and can be anywhere in the statement. You are to complete the statement by writing the correct word or words on the blank line. Sometimes there is more than one part missing in an item. In this case, you must correctly complete all missing parts to receive credit for the item.

Here are examples of completion test items with the blank line or lines in different parts of the statement. The answers are shown in ( ).

1. The two most widely spoken languages in the world are (<u>Mandarin and Spanish</u>).

2. (<u>Paris</u>) is the capital of France.

3. Houston is in (<u>Texas</u>); Boston is in (<u>Massachusetts</u>).

Here are guidelines that will help you do well when taking a completion test. Read these guidelines and use them when you take the practice completion test that follows.

- *Read the statement and think about what information could be missing.* Write possible answers on a piece of scrap paper or on the corner of the test.
- *Write the answer that best completes the statement.* Look at each of the possible answers you wrote on scrap paper or on a corner of the test. Select and write the answer you think best completes the statement.
- *Read the completed statement to be sure it is grammatically correct.* If the completed statement is not grammatically correct, your answer is probably incorrect and needs to be changed.
- *Use the length of the blank line as a clue to the length of the answer.* Short blank lines may mean that only one word is needed to complete the statement. Longer blank lines may mean that more than one word is needed to complete the statement. This guideline does not work when the length of the blank lines is the same for every test item.
- *Do not guess at an answer when there is a penalty for incorrect answers.* This is especially important for a completion test because you must *produce* the correct answer rather than just *recognize* it. Having to produce an answer increases the possibility that your guess will be incorrect.

Take the following completion test. This test is on the guidelines for taking completion tests you just learned about.

Directions   Complete each statement by writing the missing word or words on the blank line or lines. There is no penalty for incorrect answers.

1. The completed statement should be _____ correct.

2. Sometimes the answer is one word; sometimes it is _____ .

3. Read the statement and _____ about what information could be missing.

4. Guessing at the answer to a completion test item is risky because you must _____ the correct answer rather than just _____ it.

5. Use the length of the _____ as a clue to the length of the answer.

6. _____ the entire statement, including your written answer, to be sure it makes sense.

7. Write the answer that best completes the _____ .

Score your test as your teacher goes over the answers. Your score is your number correct. Enter your score in the box below to see how well you did.

My score _____
7 = Excellent
5–6 = Good
0–4 = Review the guidelines.

Essay test items require you to recall and organize information and then write answers in the form of narrative sentences or long or short essays. Here are the steps of a strategy to follow when taking an essay test.

Step 1. Some essay tests require you to answer all the items. Other essay tests require you to answer a certain number of items of your choice. Read the directions carefully to determine which option is the case.

Step 2. Read all the items carefully to determine which items you think you will be able to answer best. Begin with these items.

Step 3. Carefully reread the first item you are going to answer to learn what you must do to answer.

Some essay test items contain a *question* you must answer. Here is an example of an essay test item that has a question.

How does a study plan improve your test performance?

Other essay test items contain a *direction word* that tells you what you must do. Here is an example of an essay test item that has a direction word.

Explain how using a computer helps you in school.

Step 4. Think about the information you want to include in your answer. It is helpful to write some notes on a piece of scrap paper if allowed or on a corner of the test. You can even use the back of the test page.

Step 5. Write an outline that organizes the information into main ideas and their details. Your outline should look like this:

    Main Idea 1
      Detail a
      Detail b
      Detail c

Repeat for the other main ideas.

Step 6. Decide how much time to spend answering to the item. Leave enough time to answer all the remaining items, as well as to review your answers.

Step 7. Use your outline from Step 5 as a guide to writing your full answer. Make sure your teacher can read your writing. It is effective to begin by stating how you plan to answer the item and conclude by restating what you did to answer the item.

Step 8. Read your answer to make sure it is complete and accurate. If an item has more than one part, be sure to answer each part.

Step 9. Check your spelling, grammar, and punctuation. Teachers often deduct points for errors in these writing mechanics.

Repeat Steps 3 through 9 for each item you answer.

Answer these questions.

1. If you cannot use scrap paper, where can you write notes?

   _____

2. What does a direction word do?

   _____

3. Which items should you begin with?

   _____

4. As you organize the information to include in your answer, where should you place a detail?

   _____

5. Does every essay test item include a direction word?

   _____

6. Why should you read your answer?

   _____

Here are **direction words** often found in essay test items. Read what each direction word tells you to do.

List:	Present information as a series of numbered facts.
Summarize:	State the major points about something in a brief manner.
Relate:	Show how two or more things are related.
Explain:	Provide information to show how to do something, how something works, or to make something clear.
Evaluate:	Judge the merits of something using certain criteria.
Outline:	Present the most important information about something in a carefully organized manner.
Trace:	State a series of events in the order in which they happened.
Contrast:	Tell how two or more things are different.
Diagram:	Create a visual representation to show something.
Justify:	Provide reasons and facts in support of something.

Each of the following essay test items is missing a direction word. Write the most appropriate direction word from above to complete each item. You can use a direction word more than once.

1. _____ middle school and high school.

2. Richard M. Nixon was a controversial president of the United States._____ his performance as a president.

3. The Vietnam War was a difficult period in American history. _____ the events that led to America's involvement in this war.

4. _____ the steps to follow when solving a math word problem.

5. _____ the parts of the human circulatory system.

6. The Internet is a valuable tool. _____ how you can use it to help you complete school assignments.

Step 6 in the essay test strategy is to determine how much time to spend answering each required item. Here is how to do this.

- Determine the total time you have to complete the test.
- Determine how many items you need to answer.
- Consider how many points each item is worth. Plan to spend the most time on items that count for the most points.
- Plan to spend more time on items you find difficult than on items you find easy.
- Write in front of each item the amount of time you plan to use answering the item.
- Make sure the time you plan for answering all items is not greater than the total time you have to take the test. If the time you planned is greater than the total time, revise your plan.

Pretend that you are about to take an essay test that has four items. You must answer all items. The test counts for 100 points. The first item is worth 40 points. Each of the other three items is worth 20 points. Item 2 looks easy to you, whereas item 4 looks difficult. You have 60 minutes to take the test.

1. What is the total time you have to take the test?_____

2. For which item should you use the most time?_____

3. Write the number of minutes you plan to use to answer each item:

   Item 1_____

   Item 2_____

   Item 3_____

   Item 4_____

4. Add the minutes to find the total number of minutes you planned to use answering the four items. Write the number of minutes here._____

5. Is your total planned time greater than the total time you have to take the test?_____

6. What should you do if your planned time is greater than the time allowed to take the test?

   _____

   _____

7. If you have time remaining, what do you think would be a good use of that time?

   _____

   _____

Read the following passage about money.

Money is some type of paper bill or metal coin that people use to exchange for things they want to purchase or accept for a job they do. Most modern money consists of paper bills and coins made of copper, nickel, and other metals. Bills and coins from different countries have various appearances and a variety of names.

Money is used in several ways. The most important function of money is as a medium of exchange. This means that people will accept money in exchange for their goods and services. If money was not available as a medium of exchange, people would have to use the barter system. For example, if you wanted a new jacket, you would have to barter or trade for it by finding something the store owner would accept in exchange, perhaps some vegetables or fruit grown in your garden. Bartering can be inconvenient and time-consuming.

Money also serves as a unit of account. People relate the value of goods and services to a sum of money. The dollar is the unit of currency in the United States. *Dollars* are used to indicate price in the same way that *gallons* are used to measure volume of liquid and *miles* are used to measure distance. Some other countries and units of currency are: Japan–yen; India–rupee; South Africa–rand; Honduras–lempira; and China–yuan.

Money should be convenient to use. It should be available in pieces of standard value so that the pieces do not have to be weighed or measured individually each time they are needed. It should be carried easily so that people can transport it to purchase what they need. Money should be easily divided into units so that people can make small purchases and receive change if needed. The beads, cocoa beans, shells, and tobacco used in the past for money do not meet the criteria of convenience when applied to modern uses of money.

The barter system of trading was used by most primitive people because they learned by experience that almost everyone was willing to accept certain goods in exchange for products or services. The goods they exchanged included salt, animal hides, cattle, cloth, and articles of gold and silver. These early people used the merchandise they bartered as a medium of exchange in a manner similar to our use of money today.

The Lydians, a people who lived in what is now western Turkey, are credited with the invention of the first metal coins, sometime around 600 B.C. The bean-shaped coins they used were a natural mixture of gold and silver, called *electrum*. The electrum were stamped with a design to show that the King of Lydia guaranteed them to be of uniform size. These coins became a medium of exchange accepted by traders instead of cattle, cloth, or gold dust. When other countries recognized the convenience of the Lydian coins, they devised metal money of their own. Today's coins are modeled after the early Lydian prototypes. Modern coins, not unlike the coins of ancient Lydia, have a government-approved design and a value stamped on their face.

Paper money originated in China during the seventh century. Even though the Italian trader, Marco Polo, exposed Europeans to this Chinese innovation, Europeans could not understand how a piece of paper could be valuable. They did not use paper money until the 1600s, when banks began to issue paper bills called *bank notes* to depositors and borrowers.

The American colonists did not use paper currency. They had to buy products from the English traders with *bills of exchange*. These were documents received from English traders in exchange for goods. It was not until the Revolutionary War that the American Continental Congress issued paper money to help finance the war. From that time forward, the United States used paper money.

Today, it would be very difficult to buy and sell products available in stores without money. Paper and coin money make it easy and quick to purchase a variety of consumer goods. Imagine what your day would be like if you had to barter for lunch, gasoline, or a ticket to see a movie or sports event.

Based on the passage about money, write each of the following test items.

1. A multiple-choice item in the form of an incomplete statement followed by four answer choices.

   Statement: _____

   a. _____

   b. _____

   c. _____

   d. _____

2. A multiple-choice item in the form of a question followed by five answer choices.

   Question: _____

   a. _____

   b. _____

   c. _____

   d. _____

   e. _____

3. A true/false item.

   _____

4. A matching test with four items in the left-hand column and five in the right-hand column.

   Directions: _____

   Heading _____   Heading _____

   1. _____ _____   a. _____

   2. _____ _____   b. _____

   3. _____ _____   c. _____

   4. _____ _____   d. _____

                                         e. _____

5. A completion test item with the missing part at the end.

   _____

6. A completion test item with two missing parts.

   _____

7. An essay test item that contains a question to be answered.

   _____

8. An essay test item that contains the direction word *compare*.

   _____

9. An essay test item that contains the direction word *evaluate*.

   _____

10. An essay test item that contains a direction word you provide.

    _____

Reading Long Words

ACTIVITIES

9-1 Forming Words with Prefixes

9-2 Forming Words with Suffixes

9-3 Recognizing Prefixes and Suffixes

9-4 Forming Long Words

9-5 Dividing Multisyllable Stems: VC/CV

9-6 Dividing Multisyllable Stems: V/CV

9-7 Dividing Multisyllable Stems: VC/V

9-8 Learning about the P2SBA Strategy

9-9 Practice Using P2SBA

9-10 Using P2SBA with Science and Social Studies Words

9-11 Using P2SBA on Your Own

A **prefix** is a word part added at the beginning of a word. When added to a word, a prefix changes the meaning of the word.

For each of the following, add the prefix to the stem and write the new word that is formed. Then write another word that begins with the same prefix. The first one is done for you.

Prefix	Stem	New Word	Another Word
1. mis	count	miscount	misspell
2. sub	zero	_____	_____
3. semi	circle	_____	_____
4. un	certain	_____	_____
5. dis	appear	_____	_____
6. mid	year	_____	_____
7. re	paint	_____	_____
8. pre	view	_____	_____
9. tri	angle	_____	_____
10. im	balance	_____	_____
11. tele	phone	_____	_____
12. trans	port	_____	_____

Forming Words with Suffixes

A **suffix** is a word part added at the end of a word. When added to a word, a suffix changes the function of the word.

For each of the following, add the suffix to the stem and write the new word that is formed. Then write another word that ends with the same suffix. The first one is done for you.

Suffix	Stem	New Word	Another Word
1. play	er	player	stronger
2. hope	less	_____	_____
3. self	ish	_____	_____
4. help	ful	_____	_____
5. need	ed	_____	_____
6. friend	ly	_____	_____
7. good	ness	_____	_____
8. light	est	_____	_____
9. walk	ing	_____	_____
10. fulfill	ment	_____	_____
11. comfort	able	_____	_____
12. enjoy	ment	_____	_____

The information in the box will help you remember the meanings of a prefix and a suffix.

> **Prefix:** A word part added to the beginning of a word. When added to a word, a prefix changes the meaning of the word.
>
> **Suffix:** A word part added to the end of a word. When added to a word, a suffix changes the function of the word.

Look at the long words. Next to each long word, write the prefix if there is one, and the suffix if there is one. The first one is done for you.

Long Word	Prefix	Suffix
1. repairing	re	ing
2. weakness		
3. unaffordable		
4. remarkable		
5. misunderstood		
6. priceless		
7. unbolted		
8. wonderful		
9. helpless		
10. unprofitable		
11. disagree		
12. unhealthful		

Forming Long Words

Look at the long words in the first column. Some of the words have a prefix. Some have a suffix. Some have both a prefix and a suffix. For each word, write the prefix if there is one, the stem, and the suffix if there is one. Then write the long word in the last column. The first word is done for you.

Long Word	Prefix	Stem	Suffix	Long Word
1. uncomfortable	un	comfort	able	uncomfortable
2. smartest				
3. reword				
4. misleading				
5. unskilled				
6. premature				
7. refund				
8. disagreeable				
9. illegal				
10. hardest				
11. transplanted				
12. important				

When a stem has more than one syllable, you must divide it into separate syllables to pronounce it.

Look at these stems: *after, signal*. Each has a vowel followed by a consonant, and then a consonant followed by a vowel. This is known at the VC/CV pattern. The rule for dividing a stem that has this pattern is to divide the stem between the two consonants. The division is shown by a slash (/). Here is how to do this:

VC/CV	VC/CV
af/ter	sig/nal

Here are some stems that follow the VC/CV pattern. Draw a slash to divide each stem into two syllables.

1. winter

2. cargo

3. number

4. differ

5. submit

6. lumber

7. carpet

8. simmer

9. garden

10. napkin

11. helmet

12. under

13. Write the rule you learned for dividing stems that follow the VC/CV pattern into syllables.

_____

_____

 **9-6**

Look at these stems: *tiger, local.*

Each has a vowel and then a consonant followed by a vowel. For each of these stems, the first vowel is pronounced with the long sound. The rule for dividing a stem that has this pattern is to divide the stem after the first vowel. Here is how to do this.

V/CV   V/VC
fe/ver   lo/cal

Here are some stems that follow the V/CV pattern. For each stem the first vowel has the long sound. Draw a slash to divide each stem into two syllables.

1. cocoa   2. silent

3. basic   4. human

5. fever   6. nasal

7. labor   8. rumor

9. famous   10. climate

11. Write the rule you learned for dividing stems that follow the V/CV pattern into syllables.

_____

_____

Look at these stems: *river, habit*. Each has a vowel followed by a consonant, and then a vowel.

For each of these stems the first vowel is pronounced with the short sound. The rule for dividing a stem that has this pattern is to divide the stem between the consonant and second vowel. Here is how to do this.

VC/V   VC/V
riv/er   hab/it

Here are some stems that follow the VC/V pattern. Draw a slash to divide each stem into two syllables.

1. image

2. gravel

3. posture

4. damage

5. rigid

6. comic

7. dozen

8. petal

9. seven

10. epic

11. Write the rule you learned for dividing stems that follow the VC/V pattern into syllables.

_____

_____

A long word contains two or more syllables. **P2SBA** is a strategy for reading long words. Each letter stands for a step in the strategy. Look in the box to see what each letter in the strategy stands for.

P = Prefix
S = Suffix
S = Stem
B = Blend
A = Ask

Here is how to use the steps of the **P2SBA strategy** to read a long word:

Look for a Prefix at the beginning of the word. There may not be a prefix.

The prefix is underlined in <u>pre</u>senting. **Underline the prefix in previewing.**

> <u>pre</u>senting **1.** previewing

Look for a Suffix at the end of the word. There may not be a suffix.

> The suffix is underlined in present<u>ing</u>. **Underline the suffix in previewing.**

> present<u>ing</u> **2.** previewing

Look for the Stem. The stem is what remains after the prefix and suffix have been removed.

> The stem is underlined in pre<u>sent</u>ing. **Underline the stem in previewing.**

> pre<u>sent</u>ing **3.** previewing

Blend the parts. Separately pronounce the prefix if there is one, the stem, and the suffix if there is one. Then blend these parts of the word to pronounce the entire word. If necessary, use the phonetic respelling of the word found in a dictionary to help you pronounce any part of the word or the entire word.

Ask for help. If you still cannot read the word, ask your teacher or another student to help you.

Answer the following about the P2SBA strategy:

4. What should you look for at the beginning of a word?

   _____

5. What should you look for at the end of a word?

   _____

6. What remains after the prefix and suffix have been removed?

   _____

7. What should you blend to pronounce a word?

   _____

8. Next to each letter in the **P2SBA** strategy, write the word for which the letter stands.

   P _____

   S _____

   S _____

   B _____

   A _____

Practice Using P2SBA

Use the P2SBA strategy to read the long word that is underlined in the sentence that follows.

The findings of the experiment were <u>unspeakable</u>.

Prefix	Write the prefix, if there is one	1. _____
Suffix	Write the suffix, if there is one.	2. _____
Stem	Write the stem.	3. _____

Blend   Separately pronounce each part of the word. Then blend the parts to pronounce the entire word. Use a dictionary if you need to.

Ask   If you still cannot read the word, ask your teacher or another student for help.

4. Explain how to use the **P2SBA** strategy to read *unmanageable*.

_____

_____

_____

_____

_____

_____

_____

_____

_____

_____

_____

_____

_____

_____

_____

_____

_____

You can use **P2SBA** to learn to read long science and social studies words you find in your text-books.

1. Locate a long science word you find difficult to read.

    Write the word here. _____

Complete each step of the **P2SBA** to help you read the word you just wrote.

Prefix	Write the prefix.	_____
Suffix	Write the suffix.	_____
Stem	Write the stem.	_____
Blend	Separately pronounce each part of the word. Then blend the parts to pronounce the entire word. Use a dictionary if necessary.	
Ask	Ask for help if necessary.	

2. Now, locate a long social studies word you find difficult to read.

    Write the word here._____

Complete each step of the **P2SBA** to help you read the word you just wrote.

Prefix	_____
Suffix	_____
Stem	_____
Blend	Separately pronounce each part of the word. Then blend the parts to pronounce the entire word. Use a dictionary if necessary.
Ask	Ask for help if necessary.

Look at each of the letters in the strategy. Write what each of these letters reminds you to do.

1. P_____

2. S_____

3. S_____

4. B_____

5. A_____

6. Write a long word you find difficult to read. _____

Complete each step in the P2SBA strategy to help you read the word you just wrote. No writing is required for the last two steps.

<u>P</u>refix   7. _____

<u>S</u>uffix   8. _____

<u>S</u>tem   9. _____

<u>B</u>lend

<u>A</u>sk

10. Write four other long words you find difficult to read. Use P2SBA to help you read these words.

_____

_____

_____

_____

UNIT TEN

Spelling Long Words

ACTIVITIES

The Syllable-Building Strategy for Spelling Words

A syllable is a word or part of word spoken with a single sound of the voice. For example, the word *thermostat* contains three syllables: therm o stat.

Read the steps in the box to see how the **syllable-building strategy** is used to spell words that contain more than one syllable. You will learn how a student used each of the steps in Activity **10-2.**

Step 1. Copy the word you need to learn to spell. Be sure you copy the word correctly when you write it.

Step 2. Locate the word you need to spell in a dictionary. The dictionary you use should show words divided into syllables as well as their phonetic respellings.

Step 3. Pronounce the word. If needed, use the phonetic respelling of the word in the dictionary to help you pronounce the word. Ask your teacher for help if you still cannot pronounce the word.

Step 4. Write the word leaving a space between each syllable.

Step 5. Write and pronounce the first syllable of the word three times. Cover what you wrote and write the first syllable from memory. Look to see if you spelled the first syllable correctly. Do this again if needed until you spell the first syllable correctly. Then repeat this step for the first two syllables together, the first three syllables together if there is a third syllable, and so on. Once you have spelled the entire word correctly from memory, go on to Step 6.

Step 6. Write the word on My Personal Spelling List. (You will learn about this in Activity **10-4.)**

Step 7. Periodically review the spellings of the words you enter on My Personal Spelling List. (You will learn review strategies in Activity **10-5.)**

Answer these questions.

1. What is a syllable?

   _____

2. What can you use in a dictionary to help you pronounce a word?

   _____

3. What should you do if you still cannot pronounce the word?

_____

4. What should you do once you have spelled an entire word correctly?

_____

5. What should you do after that?

_____

Here is how a student used the syllable-building strategy to learn to spell the word *combustion*. He came across this word as he was reading his science textbook.

Step 1. The student copied the word *combustion* from the textbook. He was careful to write the correct spelling of the word. Here is what he wrote.

combustion

Step 2. The student located a dictionary that included words divided into syllables as well as their phonetic respellings. He then found *combustion* in this dictionary.

Step 3. The student did not know how to pronounce *combustion*. He used the phonetic respelling in the dictionary to help him pronounce this word. He was not able to pronounce this word even when using its phonetic respelling, so he asked his teacher for help.

Step 4. The student learned from the dictionary that *combustion* contained three syllables. He wrote *combustion* leaving a space between each syllable. Here is what he wrote:

com bus tion

Step 5. The student wrote the first syllable of *combustion* three times. He pronounced the first syllable each time he wrote it. Here is what he wrote:

com
com
com

He covered what he had written and wrote the first syllable from memory. Here is what he wrote:

com

He looked to see if he had spelled the first syllable correctly and found that he had. He then wrote the first two syllables of *combustion* together three times. He pronounced the two syllables together as he wrote them. Here is what he wrote:

combus
combus
combus

He covered what he had written and wrote the first two syllables from memory. Here is what he wrote:

combos

He looked to see if he had spelled the first two syllables correctly and found that he had not.
He again wrote the first two syllables three times, pronouncing them as he did so. Here is what he wrote:

combus
combus
combus

He covered what he had written and wrote the first two syllables from memory. Here is what he wrote:

combus

He looked to see if he had spelled the first two syllables correctly and found that he had.

He continued this procedure for the entire word *combustion*. He correctly spelled this word.

Step 6. Once the student had correctly spelled the entire word, he entered *combustion* on My Personal Spelling List. You will see how he did this in Activity **10-4**.

Step 7. The student periodically reviewed the spelling of *combustion*.

Answer these questions.

1. What was included in the dictionary the student used?

   _____

2. What did the student do when he could not pronounce *combustion* using the dictionary?

   _____

3. What did he do when he found he had not written the first two syllables of *combustion* correctly?

   _____

Follow the steps in the syllable-building strategy to spell the word *declaration*.

Step 1. Write the word *declaration* here. Be sure to spell it correctly._____

Step 2. Locate a dictionary that includes words divided into syllables and their phonetic respellings.

Step 3. Use the phonetic respelling of *declaration* to help you pronounce this word. Ask your teacher for help if needed.

Step 4. Write *declaration* leaving a space between each syllable._____

Step 5. Complete Step 5 using the space below until you have spelled *declaration* correctly. Refer back to Activities **10-1** and **10-2** as needed.

_____

_____

_____

_____

_____

_____

_____

_____

_____

Step 6. Enter the word *declaration* on My Personal Spelling List. (You will learn about this in Activity **10-4**.)

Step 7. Periodically review the correct spelling of *declaration*. (You will learn review strategies in Activity **10-5**.)

Here is how to use **My Personal Spelling List**.

> 1. In the first column, write the date you enter a word.
> 2. In the second column, write the correct spelling of the entire word.
> 3. In the third column, write the syllables of the word with a space between each syllable.
> 4. In the fourth column, write the date each time you use a review procedure to help you remember the spelling of the word.

Look at My Personal Spelling List below to see how a student named Eileen entered the word *declaration* when she used the Syllable-Building Strategy in Activity **10-3**. She entered dates in the fourth column whenever she reviewed the spelling of *declaration*. Eileen added *encyclopedia* and *fortunate* to her list along with dates she reviewed the spellings of these words.

My Personal Spelling List			
Date Entered	**Word**	**Syllables**	**Dates Reviewed**
9/20	declaration	dec la ra tion	10/14, 11/3, 12/10
10/16	encyclopedia	en cy clo ped ia	11/11, 11/28
10/29	fortunate	for tun ate	12/7

Answer these questions.

1. What should you write in the first column of My Personal Spelling List?

   _____

2. What should you write in the third column of My Personal Spelling List?

   _____

3. On what date did Eileen enter the word *encyclopedia*?

_____

4. How many times did Eileen review the word *declaration*?

_____

5. How many syllables are there in the word *fortunate*?

_____

My Personal Spelling List

Date Entered	Word	Syllables	Dates Reviewed

Here are three **review strategies** you can use to remember how to spell words. Use these strategies with words you write on My Personal Spelling List. The more difficult the word, the more often you should review its spelling.

SAY AND SPELL

Steps:

1. **Say** the word aloud.
2. Say aloud and spell each syllable
3. **Spell** the word aloud.
4. Write the word three times.

ARRANGE AND SPELL

Steps:

1. Write each letter of the word on its own one-inch square of paper. Scramble the squares.
2. **Arrange** the squares to spell the word.
3. Say the word aloud.
4. **Spell** the word aloud.
5. Write the word three times.

COMPLETE AND SPELL

Steps:

1. Write the word on a sheet of paper. Omit one or more letters when you write the word, leaving a blank space for each missing letter. Do this four more times, each time omitting a different letter or letters.
2. **Complete** each variation of the word by filling in the missing letter or letters.
3. Write the entire word.
4. **Spell** the word aloud.
5. Write the entire word three times.

1. Which review strategy would you use?_____

2. Why?

_____

_____

_____

_____

_____

Use the syllable-building strategy to spell the science word *sedimentary*.

Step 1. Write the word *sedimentary* here. Be sure to spell it correctly.

_____

Step 2. Locate a dictionary that includes words divided into syllables and their phonetic respellings.

Step 3. Use the phonetic respelling of *sedimentary* to help you pronounce this word. Ask your teacher for help if still needed.

Step 4. Write *sedimentary* leaving a space between each syllable.

_____

Step 5. Complete Step 5 using the space below until you have spelled *sedimentary* correctly. Refer back to Activities **10-1** and **10-2** as needed.

_____

_____

_____

_____

_____

_____

_____

_____

Step 6. Enter the word *sedimentary* on My Personal Spelling List.

Step 7. Periodically use one of the review strategies from Activity **10-5** to help you remember the correct spelling of *sedimentary*. Each time you do this, record the date on My Personal Spelling List.

Identify another science word that has four or more syllables whose meaning you need to learn.

Write the word here. _____

On your own paper, use the first five steps of the Syllable-Building Strategy to learn to spell the word you just wrote. Complete Step 6 by entering the word on My Personal Spelling List in Activity 10-4. Finally, complete Step 7 by recording the date on My Personal Spelling List in Activity 10-4 each time you use a review strategy to help you remember the spelling of the word.

Use the syllable-building strategy to spell the social studies word *manufacture*.

Step 1. Write the word *manufacture* here. Be sure to spell it correctly.

_____

Step 2. Locate a dictionary that includes words divided into syllables and their phonetic respellings.

Step 3. Use the phonetic respelling of *manufacture* to help you pronounce this word. Ask your teacher for help if still needed.

Step 4. Write *manufacture* leaving a space between each syllable.

_____

Step 5. Complete Step 5 using the space below until you have spelled *manufacture* correctly. Refer back to Activities **10-1** and **10-2** as needed.

_____

_____

_____

_____

_____

_____

_____

_____

Step 6. Enter the word *manufacture* on My Personal Spelling List in Activity **10-4.**

Step 7. From time to time use one of the review strategies to help you remember the correct spelling of *manufacture*. Each time you do this, record the date on My Personal Spelling List in Activity **10-4.**

Identify another social studies word that has four or more syllables whose meaning you need to learn.

Write the word here._____

On your own paper, use the first five steps of the Syllable-Building Strategy to learn to spell the word you just wrote. Complete Step 6 by entering the word on My Personal Spelling List in Activity 10-4. Finally, complete Step 7 by recording the date on My Personal Spelling List in Activity 10-4 each time you use a review strategy to help you remember the spelling of the word.

Using the Syllable-Building Strategy with Language Arts Words

Use the syllable-building strategy to spell the language arts word *publication*.

Step 1. Write the word *publication* here. Be sure to spell it correctly.

_____

Step 2. Locate a dictionary that includes words divided into syllables and their phonetic respellings.

Step 3. Use the phonetic respelling of *publication* to help you pronounce this word. Ask your teacher for help if still needed.

Step 4. Write *publication* leaving a space between each syllable.

_____

Step 5. Complete Step 5 using the space below until you have spelled *publication* correctly. Refer back to Activities **10-1** and **10-2** as needed.

_____

_____

_____

_____

_____

_____

_____

_____

Step 6. Enter the word *publication* on My Personal Spelling List in Activity **10-4**.

Step 7. From time to time use one of the review strategies to help you remember the correct spelling of *publication*. Each time you do this, record the date on My Personal Spelling List in Activity **10-4**.

Identify another language arts word that has four or more syllables whose meaning you need to learn.

Write the word here._____

On your own paper, use the first five steps of the Syllable-Building Strategy to learn to spell the word you just wrote. Complete Step 6 by entering the word on My Personal Spelling List in Activity 10-4. Finally, complete Step 7 by recording the date on My Personal Spelling List in Activity 10-4 each time you use a review strategy to help you remember the spelling of the word.

Use the syllable-building strategy to spell the mathematics word *computation*.

Step 1. Write the word *computation* here. Be sure to spell it correctly.

_____

Step 2. Locate a dictionary that includes words divided into syllables and their phonetic respellings.

Step 3. Use the phonetic respelling of *computation* to help you pronounce this word. Ask your teacher for help if still needed.

Step 4. Write *computation* leaving a space between each syllable.

_____

Step 5. Complete Step 5 using the space below until you have spelled *computation* correctly. Refer back to Activities **10-1** and **10-2** as needed.

_____

_____

_____

_____

_____

_____

_____

_____

Step 6. Enter the word *computation* on My Personal Spelling List in Activity **10-4**.

Step 7. From time to time use one of the review strategies to help you remember the correct spelling of *computation*. Each time you do this, record the date on My Personal Spelling List in Activity **10-4**.

Identify another mathematics word that has four or more syllables whose meaning you need to learn.

Write the word here._____

On your own paper, use the first five steps of the Syllable-Building Strategy to learn to spell the word you just wrote. Complete Step 6 by entering the word on My Personal Spelling List in Activity 10-4. Finally, complete Step 7 by recording the date on My Personal Spelling List in Activity 10-4 each time you use a review strategy to help you remember the spelling of the word.

Use the syllable-building strategy to spell the humanities word *entertainment*.

Step 1. Write the word *entertainment* here. Be sure to spell it correctly.

_____

Step 2. Locate a dictionary that includes words divided into syllables and their phonetic respellings.

Step 3. Use the phonetic respelling of *entertainment* to help you pronounce this word. Ask your teacher for help if still needed.

Step 4. Write *entertainment* leaving a space between each syllable.

_____

Step 5. Complete Step 5 using the space below until you have spelled *entertainment* correctly. Refer back to Activities **10-1** and **10-2** as needed.

_____

_____

_____

_____

_____

_____

_____

_____

Step 6. Enter the word *entertainment* on My Personal Spelling List in Activity **10-4.**

Step 7. From time to time use one of the review strategies to help you remember the correct spelling of *entertainment*. Each time you do this, record the date on My Personal Spelling List in Activity **10-4.**

Identify another humanities word that has four or more syllables whose meaning you need to learn.

Write the word here._____

On your own paper, use the first five steps of the Syllable-Building Strategy to learn to spell the word you just wrote. Complete Step 6 by entering the word on My Personal Spelling List in Activity 10-4. Finally, complete Step 7 by recording the date on My Personal Spelling List in Activity 10-4 each time you use a review strategy to help you remember the spelling of the word.

Use the syllable-building strategy to spell the recreation word *photography*.

Step 1. Write the word *photography* here. Be sure to spell it correctly.

_____

Step 2. Locate a dictionary that includes words divided into syllables and their phonetic respellings.

Step 3. Use the phonetic respelling of *photography* to help you pronounce this word. Ask your teacher for help if still needed.

Step 4. Write *photography* leaving a space between each syllable.

_____

Step 5. Complete Step 5 using the space below until you have spelled *photography* correctly. Refer back to Activities **10-1** and **10-2** as needed.

_____

_____

_____

_____

_____

_____

_____

_____

Step 6. Enter the word *photography* on My Personal Spelling List in Activity **10-4.**

Step 7. From time to time use one of the review strategies to help you remember the correct spelling of *photography*. Each time you do this, record the date on My Personal Spelling List in Activity **10-4.**

Identify another recreation word that has four or more syllables whose meaning you need to learn.

Write the word here._____

On your own paper, use the first five steps of the Syllable-Building Strategy to learn to spell the word you just wrote. Complete Step 6 by entering the word on My Personal Spelling List in Activity 10-4. Finally, complete Step 7 by recording the date on My Personal Spelling List in Activity 10-4 each time you use a review strategy to help you remember the spelling of the word.

10-12

1. Describe each of the seven steps in the *syllable-building strategy*.

   Step 1. _____

   Step 2. _____

   Step 3. _____

   Step 4. _____

   Step 5. _____

   Step 6. _____

   Step 7. _____

2. Describe each of the five steps in the *complete and spell* review strategy.

   Step 1. _____

   Step 2. _____

   Step 3. _____

   Step 4. _____

   Step 5. _____

3. Describe each of the four steps in the *say and spell* review strategy.

   Step 1. _____

   Step 2. _____

   Step 3. _____

   Step 4. _____

4. Describe each of the five steps in the *arrange and spell* review strategy.

   Step 1. _____

   Step 2. _____

   Step 3. _____

   Step 4. _____

   Step 5. _____

Building Vocabulary Through Reading

ACTIVITIES

As you read, you can expect to encounter words whose meanings you do not know. Learning the meanings of these words is a great way to build your vocabulary. Writers often provide a clue to the meaning of a word they think a reader might not know. One type of clue writers provide is a **definition clue**.

A definition clue is two or more words that tell the meaning of a word. Sometimes a writer presents a word and the definition clue for the word in the same sentence. Read the sentence below to see how the writer uses the definition clue *not planned* to help the reader understand that the meaning of *impromptu* is *unplanned.*

It was an *impromptu* party because I had not planned to have a party.

Other times a writer presents a word in one sentence and the definition clue for the word in the following sentence. Read the sentences below to learn how the writer used the definition clue *every last little detail* in the second sentence to help the reader understand that the meaning of *pedantic* is *a narrow focus on the trivial aspects of learning.*

Susan felt her teacher was too *pedantic.* Her teacher included every last little detail when teaching a lesson.

In each of the following sentences, a word is underlined. Read to find the definition clue provided by the writer to help the reader understand the meaning of the underlined word. Then write the definition clue.

1. Marie's <u>lyrical</u> dance performance expressed her deep emotional attachment to ballet.

   Definition Clue: _____

2. We had come to an <u>impasse</u>. We searched for an hour but there was no exit from the road.

   Definition Clue: _____

3. The great amount of damage clearly showed the <u>magnitude</u> of the earthquake.

   Definition Clue: _____

4. Herbert's English teacher told him to <u>enunciate</u> when he spoke. When Herbert got home, he practiced pronouncing words clearly.

   Definition Clue: _____

5. Elizabeth liked the fact that her new home was in <u>proximity</u> to the school. Living close to her school meant she could sleep later each morning.

   Definition Clue: _____

6. My father is known as an <u>epicure</u> because of his refined taste in food.

   Definition Clue: _____

7. Paul <u>shredded</u> last year's homework papers by tearing them into thin strips.

   Definition Clue: _____

8. Sam raised his arms in <u>triumph</u>. He couldn't help rejoicing over his victory.

   Definition Clue: _____

Sometimes a writer provides a **synonym clue** to the meaning of a word the writer thinks a reader might not know. A synonym clue is a word that has the same or nearly the same meaning as another word. Read the following sentence to learn how the writer used a synonym clue to help the reader understand that *glorious* means *grand*.

The float was *glorious* and just one part of a *grand* parade.

Other times a writer presents a word in one sentence and a synonym clue for the word in the sentence that follows. Read the following two sentences to see how the writer used the synonym clue *minimum* in the second sentence to help the reader understand that *modicum* means *minimum*.

Tyler would be happy if he experienced a *modicum* of success in his experiments. He knew that even great scientists started with *minimum* success.

In each of the following sentences, a word is underlined. Read to find the synonym clue provided by the writer to help the reader understand the meaning of the underlined word. Then write the synonym clue.

1. Harry was willing to <u>compromise</u> with Richard and actually felt quite good once they had reached an understanding.

    Synonym Clue: _____

2. The <u>fulfillment</u> of his contract was a relief. Tom felt better once his obligations under the contract had come to completion.

    Synonym Clue: _____

3. Bill's room was a <u>muddle</u>. His mother said it was a big mess because his clothes were thrown all over the floor.

    Synonym Clue: _____

4. Susan did not want to <u>intervene</u> because it was not in her nature to interfere in other peoples' business, especially because she was not part of the project.

    Synonym Clue: _____

5. Steve found the tutoring sessions to be very <u>beneficial</u>. He was sure the sessions had been helpful as he prepared for his final exams.

    Synonym Clue: _____

6. Yesterday, Carl was <u>cruel</u> to his younger sister. Afterward, he felt guilty for being unkind and apologized and gave her a hug.

   Synonym Clue: _____

7. Even when Sonia found a homework assignment to be difficult, she would <u>persist</u> and continue to work hard until she completed the assignment successfully.

   Synonym Clue: _____

8. Roberto had a natural <u>knack</u> for chess. His skill impressed everyone who saw how quickly he moved his pieces during a game.

   Synonym Clue: _____

Practice with Definition and Synonym Clues

> Definition Clue: Two or more words that tell the meaning of another word.
>
> Synonym Clue: A word that has the same or nearly the same meaning as another word.

The writer provided a definition clue or a synonym clue in each of the following sentences to help the reader understand the meaning of the underlined word. Underline the clue and circle Definition Clue or Synonym Clue to show which type of clue it is.

1. My math teacher said my work was <u>impeccable</u>. It had no flaws.

   Definition Clue   Synonym Clue

2. My friend's father rented a <u>limousine</u> to take guests to his fortieth birthday party. I wish I could ride in a fancy car driven by a chauffeur.

   Definition Clue   Synonym Clue

3. Everyone knew that Mike's strange behavior was part of his <u>eccentric</u> personality.

   Definition Clue   Synonym Clue

4. My mom called me <u>idle</u> because she said I was too lazy to do anything.

   Definition Clue   Synonym Clue

5. My uncle Bill is a <u>nomad</u>. He moves from place to place and has no special place he calls home.

   Definition Clue   Synonym Clue

6. I knew that a <u>mermaid</u> was related to the sea, but I did not know it was a legendary creature that was half woman and half fish.

   Definition Clue   Synonym Clue

A **visual clue** is a picture, drawing, or any illustration that helps the reader understand the meaning of the word the reader might not know. Most often, the visual clue is on the same page as the word. However, sometimes space does not allow this. In this case, the visual clue may be on the preceding or following page.

Read this sentence: My mother looked all over the house but could not find her *spectacles*. Examine the picture to see how a visual clue was provided to help the reader understand the meaning of *spectacles* as *a pair of eyeglasses*.

A word is underlined in each of the following sentences. Use the visual clue to help you understand the meaning of the underlined word. Then write what you think the underlined word means.

1. I have never been able to ride a <u>unicycle</u>.

Meaning of unicycle: _____

2. Our teacher asked us to stand in a <u>semicircle</u>.

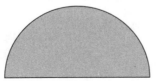

Meaning of semicircle: _____

3. I would like to be an <u>astronomer</u> when I graduate from college.

Meaning of astronomer: _____

4. The pilot said we could not take off because there was a problem with the airplane's <u>propeller</u>.

Meaning of propeller: _____

5. My <u>goggles</u> became filled with water as I swam across the pool.

Meaning of goggles: _____

6. Did you know that the most important military building in the United States was built in the shape of a <u>pentagon</u>?

Meaning of pentagon: _____

Choosing a Dictionary Definition

While reading, you will often encounter words whose meanings you do not know, but for which no clues are provided. You can use a dictionary to learn the meanings of these words. The word whose meaning you look for in a dictionary is the *entry* word. For most entry words, more than one meaning is provided.

Look at the following three meanings provided in a dictionary for the entry word *medium*.

    a. something that is in the middle
    b. a means through which something acts
    c. the conditions in which something lives or exists

For each of the sentences that follow, write the meaning of *medium* intended by the writer. Use the context in which the word was used to decide which meaning was intended by the writer.

1. The newspaper is a powerful *medium* through which to get your message across.

    _____

2. I am of *medium* height, neither too tall too short.

    _____

3. The atmosphere is a perfect *medium* for sound waves.

    _____

Respond to the following.

4. Tell why it was important to take context into account to identify the meaning of a word as used by the writer.

    _____

    _____

5. Write your own sentence using *medium* in any context you choose.

    _____

    _____

Here are four meanings of the word *flow*.

    a. to move or run smoothly with unbroken continuity
    b. to circulate
    c. to hang loosely and gracefully
    d. to derive

For each of the following sentences, write the meaning of *flow* shown above intended by the writer.

1. It is important for life that blood *flow* through the body.

_____

2. The water *flowed* quickly downstream.

_____

3. Phillip's conclusion *flowed* directly from the facts he presented.

_____

4. The silk robe *flowed* beautifully from Margaret's shoulders.

_____

Complete the following.

5. Write your own sentence using the meaning of *flow* as "to circulate."

_____

_____

6. Write your own sentence using the meaning of *flow* as "to derive."

_____

_____

7. Write your own sentence using the meaning of *flow* as "to hang loosely and gracefully."

_____

_____

8. Write your own sentence using the meaning of *flow* as "to move or run smoothly with un-broken continuity."

_____

_____

Reviewing the Meanings of Words

Once you have learned the meaning of a word, you should review the meaning of that word as often as possible. Here is a procedure you can use to do this:

- Say the word.
- Say the meaning of the word.
- Write a sentence using the word.
- Explain the meaning of the word to someone else.

Use this review procedure with each of the following words. For each word, the meaning you should use is provided.

1. Word: hustle

   Meaning: to cause or urge to proceed quickly

   Write your sentence here.

   _____

   _____

2. Word: predator

   Meaning: any animal that lives by hunting and feeding on other animals

   Write your sentence here.

   _____

   _____

3. Word: extrinsic

   Meaning: originating from the outside

   Write your sentence here.

   _____

   _____

4. Word: jargon

   Meaning: specialized language of a group

   Write your sentence here.

   _____

   _____

5. Word: opaque

   Meaning: cannot be penetrated by light

   Write your sentence here.

   _____

   _____

6. Word: casual

   Meaning: showing little interest or concern

   Write your sentence here.

   _____

   _____

7. Word: prudent

   Meaning: careful in regard to one's own interests

   Write your sentence here.

   _____

   _____

8. Word: skittish

   Meaning: restlessly active or nervous

   Write your sentence here.

   _____

   _____

You should keep a record of new words whose meanings you learn. Use the **My Vocabulary Words** form to do this. Here is how to use My Vocabulary Words.

1. Next to **Word**, write the word whose meaning you have learned.
2. Next to **Meaning**, write the meaning you have learned for the word.
3. Next to **Sentence**, write the word in a sentence using the meaning you have learned for the word.
4. Next to **Review Dates,** record the date each time you review the word and the meaning you have learned for the word.

Look at the My Vocabulary Words form below. See how a student used the form for the word *monotonous*. Identify two words whose meanings you need to learn. For each word, use a dictionary to learn its most common meaning. Then enter each word, its most common meaning, and a sentence in which you use the word. You do not have to enter review dates for this activity.

My Vocabulary Words

Word	monotonous
Meaning	not interesting
Sentence	My job at the fast food place is very monotonous.
Review Dates	2/16, 2/19, 3/2
Word	
Meaning	
Sentence	
Review Dates	
Word	
Meaning	
Sentence	
Review Dates	

Name _____

My Vocabulary Words

Word _____

Meaning _____

Sentence _____

Review Dates _____

Word _____

Meaning _____

Sentence _____

Review Dates _____

Word _____

Meaning _____

Sentence _____

Review Dates _____

Word _____

Meaning _____

Sentence _____

Review Dates _____

Word _____

Meaning _____

Sentence _____

Review Dates _____

Word _____

Meaning _____

Sentence _____

Review Dates _____

Read the following passage about mammals.

There are about 4,500 species of mammals alive today. It is believed they <u>descended</u> or came down from reptiles. There are many interesting things to know about mammals. All mammals have three <u>miniature</u> or tiny bones in their ears that <u>transfer</u> sound <u>vibrations</u> from the eardrum to the inner ear. Lions live on vast grasslands called <u>savanna</u>. Rabbits are one of the most <u>prolific</u> mammals. Mammals sure are interesting. Just take a look at the mother kangaroo carrying a joey in her pouch.

For each underlined word in the passage about mammals, place a checkmark next to one of the following: Definition Clue Provided, Synonym Provided, or No Clue Provided. Then write the meaning of the word. You may have to use a dictionary if no clue is provided.

1. descended

Definition Clue Provided   _____

Synonym Clue Provided   _____

No Clue Provided   _____

What does this word mean? _____

2. miniature

Definition Clue Provided   _____

Synonym Clue Provided   _____

No Clue Provided   _____

What does this word mean? _____

3. transfer

   Definition Clue Provided   _____

   Synonym Clue Provided   _____

   No Clue Provided   _____

   What does this word mean?   _____

4. vibrations

   Definition Clue Provided   _____

   Synonym Clue Provided   _____

   No Clue Provided   _____

   What does this word mean?   _____

5. savanna

   Definition Clue Provided   _____

   Synonym Clue Provided   _____

   No Clue Provided   _____

   What does this word mean?   _____

6. prolific

   Definition Clue Provided   _____

   Synonym Clue Provided   _____

   No Clue Provided   _____

   What does this word mean?   _____

7. Look at the Visual Clue provided for the passage about mammals on the previous page.
   What is a joey?

   _____

   _____

UNIT TWELVE

Solving Math Word Problems

ACTIVITIES

RQWQC is a strategy for solving math word problems. Each of the letters stands for one of the five steps in the strategy. Read about each step.

> **Read**   Read the problem to learn what it is about. It may be helpful to read the problem out loud, form a picture of the problem in your mind, or draw a picture of the problem. Ask your teacher to explain any terms or ideas you do not understand. Be sure you understand everything in the word problem before you go on to the next step.
>
> **Question**   Find the question to be answered. Often the question is directly stated and shown with a question mark. If the question is not directly stated, you will have to determine the question to be answered.
>
> **Write**   Write the information you need to answer the question. Check to be sure you have written all the necessary information. If allowed, cross out information not needed to answer the question. Otherwise, ignore information not needed. Sometimes all the information is needed to answer the question.
>
> **Question**   Ask yourself, "What computation(s) must I do to answer the question?"
>
> **Compute**   Set up the problem on paper and do the computation(s). Check your computation(s) for accuracy. Circle your answer.

Read to learn how RQWQC is used to solve the following problem.

> The paper factory in town has 156 full-time employees. Each employee works 40 hours a week. The factory manufactured more than 100,000 reams of paper last year. What is the total number of hours worked by the employees in one week?

Here is how RW2Q is used to solve this problem.

Read

Read the problem to learn what it is about.

By reading the problem, you learn it is about the number of hours employees of the paper factory work.

Question

Identify the question to be answered.

You learn the question to be answered is, "What is the total number of hours worked by the employees in one week?"

Write

Write the information needed to answer the question.

After crossing out or ignoring information not needed (the factory manufactured 100,000 reams of paper last year), you write the following information:

> There are 156 full-time employees.
> Each employee works 40 hours a week.

Question

What computation(s) must you do to answer the question?

You will need to multiply 156 by 40.

Compute

Do the computation(s) on paper, check for accuracy, and circle the answer.

```
   156
  ×40
  ----
   000
  6240
  ----
 (6,240)
```

Answer these questions.

1. How many steps are there in the strategy? _____

2. What should you do if you are not allowed to cross out information not needed to answer the questions?

   _____

   _____

3. Is the question to be answered always directly stated? _____

4. What should you after you complete the computation(s)?

   _____

   _____

The first step in the RQWQC strategy is to **read** the problem to learn what it is about. Read the following problem.

> It was a hot day to hold batting practice, but our team still practiced for two hours. We spent the same amount of time practicing the skills for hitting, fielding, bunting, and throwing. How much time was spent on each skill?

To say that the problem is about baseball or baseball practice is not specific enough. Upon reading the problem carefully, you learn it is about the amount of time spent on various skills during baseball practice.

Read each of the following problems and complete the statement that tells what the problem is about.

1. A transport truck can carry up to 8,000 pounds. It gets 8 miles to a gallon of gas. Today it is transporting 42-inch plasma TVs. Each TV in its carton weighs 150 pounds. How many TVs can the truck transport?

   This problem is about _____

2. Ernie is on his school's track team. Each day of the week except Sunday he runs three and a half miles to build his endurance. He then takes a short break, and he runs two more miles. How many miles does he run each week?

   This problem is about _____

3. A satellite is orbiting the earth at a speed of 14,200 miles an hour. How many miles will the satellite travel in ten minutes?

   This problem is about _____

4. Red grapes cost $2.49 a pound. Green grapes cost $3.99 a pound. You decide to buy one and a half pounds of the red grapes and one pound of the green grapes. How much change will you get when paying with a ten dollar bill?

   This problem is about _____

5. The gas tank of an automobile holds 18 gallons of gas. The car runs on 97 octane gas. The tank is 60% full. How many gallons of gas will it take to fill the tank?

   This problem is about _____

6. I don't know why, but when driving somewhere, it almost always seems like it takes less time driving back. This was actually the case yesterday. My parents, my sister, and I took a nice drive into the countryside. The drive took 2 hours and 37 minutes going, and 2 hours and 2 minutes returning later in the day. We didn't stop either time. How many minutes less did the return trip take?

7. This problem is about _____

8. Last year I ran for president of the student council. I campaigned for over a month. A total of 480 votes were cast. My opponent got 41% of the votes. How many students voted for me?

This problem is about _____

9. Our school cafeteria has 36 tables. Each table has 8 seats. Today was pizza day. Of the 412 students in the school, 240 showed up for pizza. How many empty seats were there?

This problem is about _____

The second step in RQWQC is to identify the **question** to be answered. You cannot begin to solve a problem until you identify the question. Often the question is stated as a question as in the following example:

> Lindsey finished the 100-meter dash in 16.3 seconds. Tommy finished 1.2 seconds faster than Lindsey. Julio finished 1 second behind Tommy. <u>How long did it take Julio to finish the race</u>?

Other times the question is not stated as a question but is implied, as in the following example:

> Mr. Williams grows tomatoes in his garden. He sells the tomatoes to a local grocery for $1.25 a pound. He needs $150 for some gardening equipment. <u>He needs to know how many pounds of tomatoes he has to sell to earn this much money.</u> He wants to sell the tomatoes before the price drops.

The question in this problem is: How many pounds of tomatoes must Mr. Williams sell?

After each of the following problems, write the question to be answered.

1. Debbie wondered how much snow there would be in her city in the coming December. She is trying to decide whether she should buy new boots. She found a Web site that showed that for the last three years in December, her city had experienced 16 inches, 24 inches, and 12 inches of snow, respectively. Debbie figured that the average number of snow over the past three years would be the best prediction of how much snow to expect.

   _____

2. The library at Jeffrey's school checked out 1,640 books last year. Fifteen percent of the books were returned late. How many books were returned on time?

   _____

3. Mrs. Gonzalez's class needed to raise $1,200 for a class trip. They decided to sell chocolate bars to raise the money. A school fundraising company offered to sell them chocolate bars for 80 cents each. The class decided to resell the chocolate bars for $1.20. They needed to determine how many chocolate bars they would have to order. They had one month to raise the money.

   _____

4. Jordan has a prized baseball card collection. His most valuable card is now worth $42. Jordan had only paid $14 for the card. He wants to sell it, but only if he can make at least a 100% profit. Should Jordan sell the card now?

_____

5. There are 12 boys and 18 girls in Mr. Warren's fifth-grade class. He needs to select a student as an office monitor. Mr. Warren decides the fairest way to do this is to randomly pull a name out of a hat. What are the chances that a boy will be selected? Last year a girl had been selected.

_____

6. Juice cost 50 cents a container at the school vending machine. Tyrone gets $5 a week for spending money at school. He plans to save at least $2 of this money each week to put toward a new video game. He is going to buy a container of juice each day. Tyrone wonders whether this plan will work.

_____

7. Susie is a hair stylist at the local hair salon. She is happy if she receives at least a 20% tip from each customer. Susie just finished cutting and styling Mrs. Henderson's hair. The charge for this service was $40. As Mrs. Henderson left, she handed Susie a $5 bill as a tip. Is Susie happy?

_____

8. Gaby wants to treat her friends to pizza. She calls in an order for a large plain pizza for $8.50 and a medium pizza with pepperoni and sausage for $10.80. She has $20. As she hangs up the phone, Gaby suddenly becomes concerned whether she has enough money to pay for the pizzas.

_____

The third step in RQWQC is to **write** the information you need to answer the question. It is helpful to cross out or ignore information you do not need to answer the question. The information not needed just gets in the way. Sometimes all the information presented in the problem is needed to answer the question.

Read this problem.

> Hannah went to the mall to look for a sweater. Her favorite store had 12 sweaters in her size. Each sweater cost $23. Hannah decided to buy one red sweater and one blue sweater. She also decided to buy a green sweater for her friend as a birthday gift. How much did Hannah have to pay for the three sweaters?

The problem is about buying sweaters. The question to be answered is how much Hannah will have to pay for three sweaters. The information needed to solve the problem is:

> Each sweater cost $23.
> Hannah decided to buy a red sweater and a blue sweater for herself.
> She also decided to buy a green sweater for her friend.

The information not needed to answer the question is:

> Hannah went to the mall to look for a sweater.
> The store had 12 sweaters in her size.

Read each of the following problems. For each problem identify the question that needs to be answered. Then write the information needed to answer the question. Remember it is helpful to cross out any information not needed to answer the question.

1. Sandra is baking chocolate chip cookies with her mom. They have enough ingredients to bake three pounds. Sandra and her mom want to keep one pound for themselves and share the rest equally with four of Sandra's friends. Sandra and her mom want to know how many pounds of cookies Sandra will have for each friend.

_____

_____

_____

2. Kevin wanted to record a basketball game on a blank DVD. The blank DVD cost $3.28. Gerald paid for the DVD with a five dollar bill. What is the fewest number of bills and coins Kevin could have received as change? He plans to watch the recorded game with two of his friends.

_____

_____

_____

3. Serena earned 18 points in the first round of a game, lost 11 points in the second round, and earned back 16 points in the third round. It takes 100 or more points to win the game. How many points did Serena have at the end of the third round?

_____

_____

_____

4. Tim has 73 baseball cards. His friend Hector has 46 cards. Hector's friend Thomas has 104 cards. His friend Luis has the least cards. Tim wants to have the most cards of all. He wondered how many more cards he would need to get.

_____

_____

_____

5. My science class watched the TV report about the meteoroid that was falling toward earth. It was falling at a steady rate of 12 kilometers per second. The meteoroid was now 440 kilometers from earth. We would be able to see it when it dropped another 160 kilometers. How many kilometers did the meteoroid drop during the next 20 seconds?

_____

_____

_____

6. Susie wants to take 11 of her friends to see a movie on her birthday. Each ticket costs $4.40. How much will Susie have to pay for her friends?

_____

_____

_____

7. Chuck bought a hot dog for each of his six friends. Each hot dog cost $2.25. Chuck also bought a can of soda for each of his friends at $1 a can. Chuck paid for everything with a twenty dollar bill. How much did the hot dogs cost Chuck?

_____

_____

_____

8. The school assembly took an hour. It began with Ms. Torres, the principal, making some announcements that took 10 minutes. Mr. Henderson's sixth-grade class then presented a play that took 44 minutes. Ms. Torres then used the remaining time to make final announcements. How much time did she have to do this?

_____

_____

_____

The fourth step in RQWQC is to decide what computation(s) you must do with the information needed to answer the question.

Read the following problem.

> Hector decided it was time to get in shape. He began to ride his bicycle each day. Some days he rode more than others. One day he actually rode 16 miles. Here is the number of miles Hector rode each day for the first week: 11, 8, 14, 10, 5, 16, and 11. Hector wanted to know how many miles he averaged a day.

This problem is about Hector riding his bike. The question is how many miles he rode on average each day. The information needed to solve the problem is the number of miles Hector rode each day. To answer the question, you would have to first add the miles he rode each day and then divide this sum by the number of days (7).

For each of the following problems, describe in words the computation or computations you would have to do to answer the question. If more than one computation must be done for a problem, describe the computations in the order they must be done.

1. My dad borrowed $2,000 for one year. He is going to use the money to repair our driveway. Our driveway is quite large. It is 30 feet long and 20 feet wide. The interest on my dad's loan is 12%. How much interest will he have to pay?

   _____

   _____

   _____

2. My brother bought a digital camera for $275. At the same time, he bought a flash attachment for $175. He had a store credit of $75. He had hoped to spend less than $400 for the two items. Was he successful?

   _____

   _____

   _____

3. I have worked very hard this year to achieve an average of at least 80 in math. We have had four tests so far and have one more to go. One time I scored 97 but another time 72. My other two scores were 78 and 88. What is the lowest score I can get on the final test to have an average of at least 80?

_____

_____

_____

4. Penny's family donated nine cases of canned food to the local food drive. Seven of the cases contained mixed vegetables, whereas two of the cases contained spaghetti. Each of the cases could hold four rows of six cans. Two of the cases were not full. One case of mixed vegetables contained 20 cans, and one of the cases of spaghetti contained 18 cans. How many cans of food did Penny's family donate?

_____

_____

_____

5. Ashton High School just completed its basketball season with a record of 17 wins and 6 losses. They scored a total of 1,610 points. Their opponents scored 1,540 points against them. In the games they won, Ashton scored 1,420 points, whereas their opponents scored 1,180 points. What was the average number of points by which Ashton won their games?

_____

_____

_____

6. I finally made it to the finals of the spelling bee. There were 280 contestants the first day, but 60% were eliminated. Of those remaining, another 20% were eliminated the second day. I was still in there. My mother asked me the number of contestants who would begin the third day.

_____

_____

_____

7. Bobby decided to buy a sub for lunch. He wanted a ham and swiss on white. A 12" ham and swiss sub costs $6.75. A 6" sub costs $3.75. Chips cost an additional $0.79. A large soda costs $1.50. Bobby was very hungry and wanted a 12" sub with double meat. Double meat costs an additional $1.50. Bobby had $8.25. How much more money would he need for a 12" double meat sub with chips and a large soda?

_____

_____

_____

8. It was Christine's lucky day. She was walking through the mall when she noticed a sign in the shoe store that read "SALE." A pair of shoes that she had always wanted had its original price of $35 reduced by 25%. Even better, the sign said that the new price would be reduced by an additional 10% the next day. Christine had saved $20 for a pair of shoes. Would she have enough money to buy the shoes the next day?

_____

_____

_____

The fifth and final step in RQWQC is to do the computations on paper, check them for accuracy, and circle your answer. **Do the computations for each of the problems in Activity 12-5.**

1.

2.

3.

4.

5.

6.

7.

8.

Use RQWQC to solve this problem involving fractions.

Jimmy had five books he wanted to place on a shelf. He measured the space available on the shelf and found it was 9½ inches. He selected three of the books and placed them on the shelf. The largest was 3½ inches wide, the second was 2½ inches wide, and the thinnest was 1½ inches wide. How much space was left on the shelf?

R   Read the problem. Write a statement that tells what the problem is about.

_____

_____

Q   Write the question to be answered.

_____

_____

W   Write the information needed to answer the question. Remember, it is helpful to cross out any information not needed to answer the question.

_____

_____

Q   Write a statement that tells what computation(s) you will do.

_____

_____

C   Do the computations. Circle your answer. Remember to check your computations.

Use RQWQC to solve this problem involving decimals.

Marcella's friend, Lucy, lives in California. Marcella had to ship three packages to Lucy. The first package weighed 11.3 ounces, the second weighed .56 ounces, and the third weighed 2.3 ounces less than the first. The shipping rate was 38 cents per ounce for regular shipping, and 52 cents per ounce for special handling. What shipping charge did Marcella have to pay for regular shipping?

R   Read the problem. Write a statement that tells what the problem is about.

_____

_____

Q   Write the question to be answered.

_____

_____

W   Write the information needed to answer the question. Remember, it is helpful to cross out any information not needed to answer the question.

_____

_____

Q   Write a statement that tells what computation(s) you will do.

_____

_____

C   Do the computations. Circle your answer. Remember to check your computations.

Use RQWQC to solve this problem involving percents.

There are 374 students at Royal Oak Junior High School. Mr. Harrison, the principal, was concerned about poor attendance. He started a program to reward good attendance. During the week before he started the program, 82 students were absent at least once. During the first week of the program, this number dropped to 71. Mr. Harrison decided that he would consider his program a success when the number of students absent at least once during a week was less than 40% of the number absent during the week before the program began. How low will the number of students absent during a week have to be for Mr. Harrison to consider the program a success?

R   Read the problem. Write a statement that tells what the problem is about.

_____

_____

Q   Write the question to be answered.

_____

_____

W   Write the information needed to answer the question. Remember, it is helpful to cross out any information not needed to answer the question.

_____

_____

Q   Write a statement that tells what computation(s) you will do.

_____

_____

C   Do the computations. Circle your answer. Remember to check your computations.

Use RQWQC to solve this problem involving proportions.

Our school cafeteria sells pints of both plain milk and chocolate milk. Last week students bought a total of 678 pints of milk. Mrs. Johnson, the school dietician, is interested in knowing the relative popularity of the two types of milk. She found out that the ratio of plain milk sold to chocolate milk sold is 5 to 3. She is ordering a total of 752 pints of milk for next week to be sure she has enough. How many pints of chocolate milk should she order?

R   Read the problem. Write a statement that tells what the problem is about.

_____

_____

Q   Write the question to be answered.

_____

_____

W   Write the information needed to answer the question. Remember, it is helpful to cross out any information not needed to answer the question.

_____

_____

Q   Write a statement that tells what computation(s) you will do.

_____

_____

C   Do the computations. Circle your answer. Remember to check your computations.

Use RQWQC to solve this problem involving interest.

Amanda received gifts of $500 from her Aunt Sally and $200 from her Uncle Bob on her sixteenth birthday. She already had a savings account with a balance of $2,200. Amanda decided to open a separate savings account with the two gifts and let the money earn interest. The bank adds 5% interest to her account every six months. Amanda wants to know how much money she will have to add to her balance after two and one half years to bring it to $1,000.

R Read the problem. Write a statement that tells what the problem is about.

_____

_____

Q Write the question to be answered.

_____

_____

W Write the information needed to answer the question. Remember, it is helpful to cross out any information not needed to answer the question.

_____

_____

Q Write a statement that tells what computation(s) you will do.

_____

_____

C Do the computations. Circle your answer. Remember to check your computations.

Show what you have learned by creating and solving you own math word problem. Be certain your problem includes a question to be answered and some information not needed to answer the question. Write your problem here.

_____

_____

_____

_____

R Read the problem. Write a statement that tells what the problem is about.

_____

_____

Q Write the question to be answered.

_____

_____

W Write the information needed to answer the question. Remember, it is helpful to cross out any information not needed to answer the question.

_____

_____

Q Write a statement that tells what computation(s) you will do.

_____

_____

C Do the computations. Circle your answer. Remember to check your computations.

COMPANION CD-ROM ASSESSMENT

Dr. Mangrum and Dr. Strichart have developed a CD-ROM assessment that evaluates students' use of the skills and strategies taught across all units of this book. The assessment can be used to plan instruction and assess students' progress. Together, the activities in this book and the CD-ROM assessment provide a complete study skills program that can be used as a curriculum for study skills classes, as well as with individuals and small groups of students.

An unlimited number of students can take the assessment on their own any number of times you wish. For each administration, students can take the entire assessment or any unit or units you select. An audio component allows students who have poor reading skills to hear any item read aloud. Results are automatically scored and saved as files. Four types of reports are immediately available for viewing and/or printing: an individual diagnostic profile, an individual narrative report, an individual instructional objectives report, and a class diagnostic profile.

The CD-ROM assessment can be used with all Windows and Mac systems and is available in both stand-alone and network versions. It is provided by Mangrum-Strichart Learning Resources. You can learn more about the assessment at their Web site: www.mangrum-strichart.com or by calling their toll-free number: 866-409-0585.